GEORGES BIZET

GEORGES BIZET

BY

MARTIN COOPER

GREENWOOD PRESS, PUBLISHERS
WESTPORT, CONNECTICUT

The Library of Congress cataloged this book as follows:

Cooper, Martin, 1910–
    Georges Bizet. Westport, Conn., Greenwood Press ₍1971₎

    136 p. music. 23 cm.

    Reprint of the 1938 ed.
    Bibliography : p. 136.

    1. Bizet, Georges, 1838–1875.

ML410.B62C77 1971   780'.924 [B]   71–138216
ISBN 0–8371–5571–1   MARC

Library of Congress   71 ₍4₎   MN

Originally published in 1938 by Oxford University Press,
London, New York, Totonto

Reprinted with the permission of Oxford University Press, Inc.,
New York

Reprinted by Greenwood Press, Inc.

First Greenwood reprinting 1971
Second Greenwood reprinting 1976

Library of Congress Catalog Card Number 71-138216

ISBN 0-8371-5571-1

Printed in the United States of America

71-8950

For Ralph

CONTENTS

CHAPTER I

THERE appear now and again in the history of music, as of the other arts, figures who achieve a reputation by a single work, sometimes a genuine masterpiece, sometimes a mere novelty whose *succès de scandale* wins notoriety for the composer. These reputations are often incomplete, for it is rare to find any artist of merit who can strike off a single immortal work and devote the rest of his life to the production of really worthless music. Time more often reveals that the lesser-known works of such men show at least some degree of talent and originality and may also serve to explain and illumine the genesis and true value of the single work by which they have become famous.

Georges Bizet does in a certain sense stand alone, in that he died extremely young and immediately after the production of the masterpiece which has made his name famous; and it is therefore natural that his earlier works, in most of which he had hardly achieved complete maturity, should have been been passed over entirely in favour of *Carmen*, which was not only his greatest and most successful work but also the first in which he achieved completely mature individuality. Not even in his case, however, are the earlier and less known works completely negligible: and I hope to be able to show that *Carmen*, far from being a sudden and inexplicable ebullition of genius, is really the natural and logical production of a composer who, starting with *Les Pêcheurs de Perles* and *La Jolie Fille de Perth*, progressed naturally through *Djamileh* and *L'Arlésienne* to his first, and unhappily his only, masterpiece.

Alexandre-César-Léopold Bizet was born on October 25, 1838, in Paris. His father was a teacher of singing and his mother was sister of the pianist Delsarte, so that Georges Bizet—as he was always called, after a favourite godfather—was born into a family at least conscious of music. At the age of nine he entered the Paris Conservatoire as a pupil of Marmontel (pianoforte) and Zimmermann (composition). In 1849, at the age of eleven, he won the *prix de solfège*; in 1851 the second piano prize; in 1852 the first piano prize; in 1854 the second prize for fugue and organ; in 1855 the first prize for fugue and organ. In 1856 Bizet entered for the Prix de Rome and was placed second; in the same year, he won, with Lecocq, a prize offered by Offenbach for an operetta, Bizet's and Lecocq's settings of the same libretto being given on alternate nights at the theatre. In 1857 he entered again for the Prix de Rome and won the prize.

Already in 1855, when he was only seventeen, he had given amazing proof of his powers in a Symphony in C major, written in the single month of November. It was not profoundly original, but it showed at the worst a great imitative faculty, a most unusual grasp of design and an unfailing sense of

style, though the style was often that of his models.
The first subject of the first movement

Ex.1

shows the influence of Beethoven, the second

Ex.2

that of Mozart. The orchestration is already masterly
in its neatness and balance, there is a nervous brilliance and, above all, an astonishing sureness of
touch in the crisp, semi-comic cut of some of the
phrases.

Ex. 3

The slow movement, particularly, would be hard
to parallel in the productions of seventeen-year-olds
without turning to the works of Mozart or Mendelssohn. Patently inspired by Rossini, the elegiac oboe
theme accompanied by the violas' *pizzicato* is abso-

lutely mature in its suave emotion, a certain evoca-
tive languor and an elegance which never falters.

Ex.4

The last movement has something of the *brio* of
Haydn and Rossini. A short, march-like episode,
very effective on the wood-wind, was used again
later as an entr'acte in *Don Procopio* and foreshadows
already the mock-soldier gamins of *Carmen*. But
Bizet makes fullest play with the enchanting

Ex.5

modulating and ornamenting it with the obvious delight of an accomplished craftsman.

At nineteen Bizet had had the very best musical education that Paris could give him, and he had won the blue ribbon of musical prizes. At the Conservatoire he had studied with Zimmermann, Marmontel, Halévy and Gounod. Zimmermann was a pupil of Cherubini, and therefore in the purest scholastic tradition: he had taught Alkan, Marmontel, Ambroise Thomas and Gounod, who married Zimmermann's daughter and took over Bizet's instruction from his father-in-law. Marmontel was a brilliant pianist, who trained a whole generation of virtuosi and he had a particularly high opinion of Bizet's talent. Halévy had great dramatic gifts as a composer, and he developed the same gifts in his pupil. But the atmosphere of the Conservatoire was not that of the rest of Paris. The musical world in which Bizet grew up was dominated by a few great figures. The chief of these were Meyerbeer, whose *Robert le Diable* (1831) and *Les Huguenots* (1836) had had an enormous success; and Rossini whose *William Tell* (1829) had made him a fortune. Bellini and Donizetti were the best of a bad lot of Italian operatic composers whose works drew crowds every night to the Théâtre des Italiens, almost the most popular theatre in Paris. Verdi became a figure in Parisian musical life in the Fifties, when he wrote his *Vespri Siciliani* and *Simone Boccanegra* for the Opéra, but he was regarded as a composer of emphatically the second rank. Paris in these days of the Second Empire was pleasure-mad. It was an era of great material brilliance and luxury: and the public, who found Meyerbeer profound, terrible and comparable with Michelangelo, was really met on its own level by the sparkle and gaiety of Offenbach and Auber. This was the atmosphere into which Bizet was born, and these were the rulers of musical taste. There was hardly a performance of Beethoven, Schumann or even Mendelssohn: Berlioz was a wild eccentric with a small following, and Wagner a mere name of horror or contempt. Gounod was struggling to get a hearing: but *Faust* did not appear until 1859, and his earlier operas, *Sapho, La Nonne Sanglante, Le Médecin malgré lui*, had no popular success. Music must be brilliant and theatrical at all costs if it was to gain a hearing. Chamber music was practically non-existent and the concert hall was dominated by a few great virtuosi, Liszt, Thalberg, or Paganini. Vocal music meant opera and the song, as we know it, was unknown, drawing-room romances taking its place. Bizet had learnt a more serious conception of music at the Conservatoire: but he was young, full of vitality and ambition, and inevitably influenced by the musical atmosphere of Paris. He was bright and intelligent, without having any definitely intellectual pretensions: popular and affectionate, though quick-tempered: loving brilliance and charm rather than profundity; frankly ambitious and not over-burdened with idealism of any description. Physically, his most remarkable feature was a head of light curly hair. He was slight in build and not very strong, though energetic. A picture of him by a fellow-pupil in Rome shows him with myopic but vivacious eyes, a good oval-shaped face and a rather small, pursed mouth. Later in life he

6

grew a thick beard and bad eyesight forced him to wear spectacles.

Bizet set out for Rome with several of his fellow-students—painters and architects—and travelled in a leisurely way: for they had no need to hurry. The Prix de Rome had been founded by Louis XIV to enable young French sculptors and painters to study in Rome at the expense of the French government. It was only in 1805 that the Prix de Rome was extended to musicians. The prize-winners were housed at the Villa Médicis in Rome, and were under the supervision of a director, whose personality determined to a great extent the value for the young artist of the life in Rome and Bizet was fortunate in having as his director the painter Ingres. Strictly, the five years were divided into two years in Rome, one in Germany, and two in Paris; but this regulation was elastic and different prize-winners arranged their times in different ways. Berlioz, for example, spent rather less than his statutory time in Rome and returned directly to Paris without visiting Germany; while Gounod spent his two years in Rome and more than the statutory year in Germany, only returning to Paris after four years' absence. The only fixed rule for musicians was that they should produce and send home to the Conservatoire a yearly composition or *envoi* by which their progress could be judged. However, neither *envoi* nor the exact apportioning of his five years worried Bizet at the moment: and on his way to Rome he took the opportunity of acquainting himself with a part of his own country of which he had hitherto seen nothing. The letters which he wrote home to his family during the next

7

three years are an excellent guide to his personality and its development, both artistic and moral: and their picture of the man is true not only for those years, but, with very few exceptions, for the rest of his life.

Travelling by Lyons, Vienne, Valence, Orange, Avignon, Nîmes, Arles, Marseilles, Toulon, Nice, Genoa, Pisa, Lucca, Pistoia, Florence, Perugia, and Terni, he arrived in Rome on January 28, 1858. From Toulon he wrote that

> ' the spectacle of nature is something so unknown to me that I am quite incapable of analysing my impressions.'

He is contemptuous of the slovenliness and squalor of Italy, and horrified by the low standard of musical taste:

> ' Bad taste poisons Italy. It is a country quite lost artistically. Rossini, Mozart, Weber, Paër, Cimarosa, are unknown, despised or forgotten here.'

But his attention was soon diverted inward, to his own musical powers and feelings. At first he is confident and clear of his gifts. In April he wrote:

> ' I have plenty of hope for my career. I shall probably have much less talent and less firm convictions than Gounod: as things stand at present that means a chance of success.'

Ambition was clearly to the fore here, and not too scrupulous:

> ' I am decidedly meant for comedy (*musique bouffe*) and give myself up to that entirely',

he writes in June: but in the autumn the first flush of his excitement and confidence had faded and we find him more serious.

'I have become very hard to please,' he writes in September, 'and that means that in spite of my very great natural facility I don't go faster than the rest, rather the opposite.'

Rome, too, so poor musically, was beginning to affect him through his eyes:

'I feel my artistic affections growing stronger. Comparison of painters and sculptors with musicians plays a large part. All the arts are connected, or rather there is but one art. Express your thought on canvas, in marble, or in the theatre, it is all one; the thought is the same. I am more than ever convinced that Mozart and Rossini are the two greatest musicians. Admiring Beethoven and Meyerbeer with all my faculties, I feel by nature more inclined to art that is pure and easy rather than dramatic and passionate. Thus, in painting, Raphael is the same as Mozart: Meyerbeer feels as Michelangelo felt. Don't think me narrow. On the contrary, I have come to recognise Verdi as a genius, but a genius set in the most deplorable path imaginable.'

Two months later he develops this point:

'Hitherto I have wavered between Mozart and Beethoven, Rossini and Meyerbeer. Now I know what to adore. There are two sorts of genius: the natural (*génie de la nature*) and the rational (*génie de la raison*). Although admiring enormously the second of these, I will not conceal from you that the first has all my sympathies. Yes, I have the courage to prefer Raphael to Michelangelo, Mozart to Beethoven, Rossini to Meyerbeer. ... I do not put one species above another; that would be absurd: it is merely a matter of taste,

9

one class of ideas exercising a stronger attraction on me than another. When I see the Last Judgement, when I hear the *Eroica* symphony, or the fourth act of the *Huguenots*, I am moved, surprised, and have not enough eyes, ears, and intelligence for my admiration. But when I see the School of Athens, the Dispute of the Blessed Sacrament, the Virgin of Foligno, when I hear *Figaro* or the second act of *William Tell*, I am completely happy, I feel a sense of well-being and complete satisfaction, I forget everything.'

This is perhaps superficial as a piece of aesthetics, but it describes a sincere feeling and a sincere desire to get at the truth. His admiration of the natural and spontaneous in music did not blind him to the dangers of facility.

'I distrust my facility', he wrote in January 1859. 'There are ten intelligent fellows here who will never be more than mediocre artists, simply because of the fatal confidence with which they abandon themselves to their great natural cleverness. Cleverness in art is almost indispensable, but it only ceases to be a danger when the man and the artist are formed. I don't want to write *chic* music, I must have ideas before I start composing: that was not the way I used to write in Paris. The result is a kind of paralysis which I shall only conquer completely in a year or two.'

During this first year in Rome questions of money and worldly ambition played a certain part in Bizet's letters.

'I don't need to tell you', he writes on one occasion, 'my pleasure in hearing that money affairs are not too bad. Set your mind at rest: when I am back in Paris I hope to look after these

interests as well as everything else: one must think of everything in this world.'
And in his New Year letter, enumerating what he wishes for his parents for the year to come (1859), he writes:

' Then I shall add a hope that money, that pretty metal to which we are all subject, shall not be too lacking. I have my own little plan about that. When I have 100,000 francs (that is to say, the assurance of a livelihood), father will give no more lessons, nor will I. We will begin the life of *rentiers*, which will do us no harm. Two little successes with comic operas will bring in 100,000 francs; that is nothing. A success like the *Prophète*** brings in nearly a million. So it is not a castle in the air.'

During 1859 Bizet was consolidating his own musical opinions and working out his own individual style.

' I feel certain dramatic fibres developing in me. I am writing Italian music. I mean by that, good Italian music—Rossini, Paër, half Donizetti, a quarter of Bellini, a tenth of Verdi, a hundredth of Mercadante, and so on!'

Verdi, as we have seen before, and shall see again, was to be a difficult problem to Bizet.

' Verdi is a man of great talent, who lacks the essential quality which makes a great master-style. But he has wonderful outbursts of passion. The passion is brutal, it is true: but better a passion of this kind than none at all. His music is sometimes exasperating, never boring. In fact, I cannot understand the enthusiasts and detractors he has aroused. As far as I can see, he

* Opera by Meyerbeer, 1849.

11

deserves neither the one nor the other.'
Nevertheless, Bizet was fascinated by Verdi, whose
name recurs again and again in the next few years,
until his influence was finally and violently exorcised. Of Gounod, whom he had known as a
teacher and friend in Paris, Bizet was admiring
but rather distrustful at this time.
'What a sympathetic nature! And how happily
    one submits to the influence of his warm imagina-
    tion! Art is a priesthood for him: he has said so
    himself.'
But a few months later Bizet had come to realise
the danger of this submission.
'Gounod is essentially an original composer:
    if one imitates him one can only remain in the
    position of a pupil.'
A shrewd observation which Bizet nevertheless
found it difficult to remember and act upon.
He was busy finding the libretto for the opera
which he wished to compose as his first *envoi*, and
he found it difficult work, as he told his parents.
'You attribute the recent failures of our best
    composers' operas to bad libretti; you are right,
    but there is another reason—namely, that none
    of these composers has a whole talent. Some
    (Massé, for example) lack style and breadth of
    conception: others (David, I imagine) lack musical
    training. The greatest are lacking in the only
    means a composer has of making himself under-
    stood by the public nowadays: the *motif*, which
    is mistakenly called the idea. One can be a great
    artist without having *motif*, and then one must
    give up hope of money and a popular success:
    but one can also be a superior person and possess

this precious gift, as witness Rossini. He is the greatest of the lot because, like Mozart, he has all the qualities—elevation, style, and finally *motif*. I am quite convinced of this theory, and that is why I have hopes. I know my job very well, I am never commonplace, and finally I have discovered this talisman which is so sought after. In my opera I have a dozen *motifs*, really good ones, rhythmic and easy to remember, without making any concession to my taste.' (*sic*.)

The mysterious *motif* is something perilously near catchiness, and it is far from certain that Bizet made no concessions in order to obtain the talisman.

This was later, though. The opera of which he wrote now, *Don Procopio*, was innocent of all meretriciousness. He had found the libretto in a secondhand bookshop in Rome, and he set the old-fashioned comedy, which is a variation of the story of *Don Pasquale*, to a music which is little more than a skilful and charming pastiche of the Italian comic style of a generation earlier. From Paris he received the following report, signed by Ambroise Thomas.

' . . . this work is distinguished by its ease and brilliance, its bold and youthful style, qualities precious for the comic genre for which the composer shows a marked inclination. We are obliged, however, to censure M. Bizet for having written an *opera buffa* when the regulations demanded a mass. We would remind him that the most light-hearted natures acquire, in the meditation and interpretation of things sublime, a style which is indispensable even in light compositions and quite essential in any work which is to live.'

When Bizet left Paris he had been given a letter of introduction to Mercadante by Carafa, an old and not very distinguished Italian composer who held a post at the Conservatoire. In the autumn of 1859 Bizet and several of his friends at the Villa Médicis planned a visit to Naples, where Mercadante lived. They enjoyed themselves sightseeing and wandering round the town, until several of them fell ill, probably from some form of food-poisoning, and one of their party died, which cast a gloom over the expedition. It was not until his last evening in Naples that Bizet remembered Carafa's letter to Mercadante. It was not sealed, and from curiosity Bizet opened it and read:

' The young man who will hand you this letter has studied excellently. He has won the first prizes at our Conservatoire. But in my opinion he will make a never theatrical composer, as he has not a ha'porth of the divine fire in him (*perche non ha estro per un coglione*).'

After reading this, he decided not to call on Mercadante: but he seems to have been more amused than offended, and he probably had too much self-confidence to be upset by Carafa's judgement of him.

He was growing up during 1859, not without some of the pains and disillusionments which all sensitive people experience as they emerge from childhood.

' The older I grow ', he writes on one occasion, ' the more the idea of death terrifies me. It is not very creditable to my philosophy, but it is an emotion I cannot control.'

His first encounter with death, in Naples, was evidently a shock to him:

14

'Life is not all made up of happiness, and if everything has been easy for me hitherto, the same is not true of those I love. It's odd, but one would think that my friendship carries bad luck with it. I have noticed it for some years, and have my own ideas about it all, but I shan't develop them to you as I know you are sceptical about the whole thing. All the same it is strange.'

From Naples again, where he may well have seen some of the less pleasing sides of ecclesiastical life, he writes:

'Odd that the stronger my Christian beliefs become the more I detest those entrusted with the teaching of them. Luckily one can love God without loving the priests.'

Towards the end of the year he wrote something like a report of himself for his parents, dated Rome, November 26:

'As regards the fair sex I become less and less the *chevalier français*: I see nothing in that attitude but a satisfaction of *amour propre*. I would willingly risk my life for a friend but should think myself a fool if I lost a hair of my head for a woman. I say all this only to you because, if it got known, it would damage my future success. I have changed a lot. I don't care any longer for cakes or ices or sweets (except *marrons glacés*). I have become *une petite perfection*. The only thing that is quite unchanged is my quarrelsomeness; a jostling in the street or a stare, and brrrrrrrr, off I go. However, I do my best to improve; but it is hard, very hard.'

Italian life was making him slightly cynical, as it has often made young northerners, whose principles and beliefs are apt to be melted by a warm sun, warm glances, and fiery wine: but the cynicism was not very deep and the tone of Bizet's letters, as that of most sensitive and emotional young men, depended to a great extent on his mood of the moment. In spite of the 'strengthening of his religious beliefs' (October 1859), he wrote five months later (March 3, 1860) à propos of his second *envoi*:

'The simplest thing to do is to complete my *envoi* by a *Credo*. This part of the mass contains drama and action as well as religious feeling. The *Resurrexit* and *Ascendit*, etc., etc., would allow me to desert Christian sentiments a little in favour of action and drama. But that does not fit in with my ideas: I don't want to write a mass before I can write it well, that is to say, as a Christian. So I have chosen a strange way of reconciling my ideas with the exigencies of the Academy regulations. I am asked for religious music: very well, religious music it shall be, but pagan religious. Horace's *Carmen Seculare* has attracted me for a long time. . . . To tell the truth, I am more pagan than Christian. I have always read the Ancients with enormous pleasure, while in Christian writers I have found nothing but system, egoism, intolerance, and a complete absence of all artistic tastes. Needless to say, I except the works of Saint Paul and Saint John.'

In June he writes:

'I believe that Voltaire did more for liberty by his carping (*en frondant*) than Jean-Jacques by his philosophising.'

Rome was a good deal more attractive to Bizet in its pagan than in its Christian aspect; and his whole nature was set naturally towards the clear brilliance and charm of Voltaire rather than the enervating emotionalism of Jean-Jacques. Gounod was the strongest pull in the other direction, but in January 1860 Bizet seems to have been rather impatient with him.

'Gounod doesn't write to me any more. What makes it all the more absurd is that when he sees me again he will weep tears of tenderness—and so shall I, since nothing is more infectious than friendship, feigned or otherwise: it is so alluring and so rare.'

Nevertheless he includes Gounod in his musical enthusiasms, contrasting with a colleague at the Villa Médicis who liked 'Donizetti, Verdi, Mercadante and Co' his own favourites—Mozart, Rossini, Meyerbeer, Beethoven, Mendelssohn and Gounod. In June he writes comparing Gounod with Verdi:

'Gounod alone is a man: after him there is nobody. Verdi, they say, won't write any more: and if he did, I doubt whether he would often recover such strokes of genius as are contained in *Trovatore*, *Traviata*, and Act IV of *Rigoletto*. He is a fine artist by nature spoiled by negligence and cheap success.'

Bizet little guessed that when Verdi produced his greatest work he himself would have been dead for some years.

Meanwhile, his second *envoi* was maturing. The *Carmen Seculare* came to nothing and, still unable to face a religious text, Bizet arranged with a French acquaintance in Rome the text of a cantata based on the *Lusiades* of Camoëns, and entitled *Vasco da Gama*.

'I believe that I am making immense progress. I find it easy to work over a second time what I have written, and I know the worth of my work— two good symptoms. . . . I feel that every step is a step forward. Let us hope there will be no more hold-ups; the very good is so difficult that a whole lifetime is not enough for the achieving of it.'

His health was never too good and he had complained soon after his arrival in Rome that it was no better:

'My health is still as poor as in Paris, though my appetite has grown.'

Now he writes of the tryingness of the weather:

'The *scirocco* has an unbelievable effect on one's nerves. You know me and you know that I am not naturally nervy. Well, on *scirocco* days I can't touch *Don Juan*, *Figaro* or *Così fan tutte*. Mozart's music affects me too directly and makes me really very unwell. Certain things of Rossini have the same effect: but oddly enough Beethoven and Meyerbeer never go so far as that. As for Haydn, he has sent me to sleep for some time past, as does old Grétry—not to speak of Boïeldieu, Nicolo, etc., who no longer exist for me.'

He had obtained leave to stay a third year (1860) in Rome, instead of the statutory year in Germany, in order to be with his friend Ernest Guiraud, who had won the Prix de Rome for that year. In spite of his admiration for Beethoven and Mendelssohn (and later, Schumann) the seriousness and academic learning, the comparative colourlessness and dryness of much of German music in the 'Fifties and 'Sixties must have repelled Bizet. Essentially a Latin and a Parisian, he probably felt half-overwhelmed, half bored and depressed by the thought of Germany and German music: and the clarity and warmth of the Italian climate, the beauty of the Italian landscape and buildings had a greater attraction, and probably a more wholesome effect, than the austerer climate and more intellectual pleasures of Germany on a composer whose genius it was, according to Nietzsche, to *meditérraniser la musique*.

In July 1860 he was planning his return to Paris. 'Being near you, even with you, has one disadvantage. I have got into extremely free and easy ways here, which I could not give up, as I should be obliged to do if they caused you anxiety and inconvenience. If you are worried when I come in late, I am obliged to come in earlier and so give up that freedom without which an *homme de cœur* cannot be happy. As for the people who will come and see me, that raises no difficulty. I don't care for women of easy virtue, and even if I occasionally amuse myself with them, I don't value them enough to wish to see them in my own house. . . . If I insist on a separate key it is as much for your sakes as my own, believe me. I don't want to inconvenience you or to be inconvenienced myself.'

A month later he was on his way home, reluctant to leave Rome but aware now of the necessity of a break with these ' free and easy ways ' of his student days.

'I have told you of my determination not to return to Rome: a host of reasons have forced me to make this resolution, money being the least important of all. I have been getting too accustomed to this independent life, and have formed habits which I must break. There is no doubt about it, it is not fortunate to be too happy.'

But Bizet could not foresee the bombshell which was to greet him in Venice—the news of his mother's very serious illness. Ernest Guiraud, with whom he was travelling, only just prevented him from strangling a gondolier in an access of rage and misery when he read the letter. He hurried back to Paris as fast as possible, but failed to get there in time, and his mother died before he had seen her again.

The return to Paris after three years' absence was thus made doubly difficult and depressing. He had now to start the regular, humdrum life of a musician dependent on music for his livelihood. The state pension attaching to the Prix de Rome continued for another two years: but the free board and lodging of the Villa Médicis were no longer there, and Paris was a great deal more expensive than Rome. *Vasco da Gama*, his *envoi* for 1859, received a good report from Halévy, who nevertheless added a warning.

'We urge the composer to be on his guard against certain harmonic boldnesses which may sometimes be qualified as roughnesses.'

To the modern ear, *Vasco da Gama* would call only too little for such a stricture. The poem, as Bizet himself admitted, was appalling: and the music was perfunctory. The first of the four movements shows the Portuguese fleet setting out from Lisbon (soprano solo and chorus); the second is a *bolero d'amour* sung by the young Leonard (soprano) (this was the first appearance of a melody of which

Bizet made use all through his life, as Gluck used the melody whose final version was the *Che puro ciel* of *Orfeo*). The third movement represents a storm conjured up by the giant Adamastor (six basses!), who is opposed to the Portuguese expedition: and the last movement is a full-scale choral prayer, in the Meyerbeerian manner, giving thanks to God for delivery from the storm.

Ex.6

Dieu dont la main Sau - va Mo - ï - se
a - vec tous ses en - fants des gouff - res é - cu meux,
Toi qui les con - dui - sis vers la ter - re pro - mi - se
Ah! gui - de - nous, sau - ve - nous comme eux.

The *envoi* for 1860 consisted of two symphonic movements which were both incorporated in later works, and will be dealt with in their respective places. In their original version Bizet entitled them *Marche funèbre* and *Scherzo*.

CHAPTER II

THE letters to his family and the *envois* which he sent from Rome to the Conservatoire give us a fairly clear picture of Bizet's character, both as a man and as a musician, after his time in Rome. In recent years a violent attack has been made on him. He has been represented as a fundamentally mediocre personality, typically bourgeois in his anxiety to make a financial success of his music, with no desire for a wide or cultured philosophy of life and possessed of a knack for gauging popular taste rather than of any clearly defined or developed musical character. I believe this to be quite unjust, and to be the more dangerous for the fact that it is based on certain traits in Bizet's character and certain passages in his letters which lend a specious colour to it. The German romantic ideal of the artist, propagated in France by César Franck, Vincent d'Indy, and the Franco-Wagnerians, is one to which Bizet never wished, and would never have been able, to conform. His genius was not for philosophical profundity or religious ecstasy, not for an ideal or mystical purity, not even, perhaps, for long-sustained seriousness. As a German critic, Adolph Weissmann, has put it, he was an instinctive musician (*instinktiver Musiker*) and a master of small forms (*Feinkünstler*). He was not bound by any ties of allegiance to a particular school or doctrine: without being a revolutionary, he had it in him to be an innovator, but an innovator of that particularly

French type, who, like Rameau and Fauré, instinctively innovate within the traditional forms. Like the Mozart he so adored, he was not, apart from his music, in any way a remarkably unusual character: and like all the artists up to and including Beethoven, he felt no degradation in working to a commission. He was obliged to live by his music and he could not afford entirely to disregard popular taste and the wishes of those in whose power it lay to make his career. There was no fine intransigence about him: he accepted situations as he found them and tried to exercise, within the limits imposed by circumstances, the maximum of his originality and musical invention. If in the letters from Rome the desire for a brilliant popular and financial success is rather ominously to the fore, it must be borne in mind that Meyerbeer, Rossini, and Offenbach were the chief figures in the musical world in which Bizet had grown up; and it would have been strange if their glittering successes had not stirred a germ of emulation in a young man the débuts of whose career gave him every reason to suppose himself a possible successor to these idols. The great works of all time are not created, as a rule, by these sensible, pliable characters: but it is wrong to dub them cowards and traitors to their art. They act as liaison officers between the public and the greatest artistic creators, raising steadily, though perhaps often imperceptibly, the standard of general appreciation and, by the charm and excellence of their workmanship in familiar forms, preparing the way for the more violent and difficult phases which appear in the development of every art. The purification of the French operatic stage in the second half of the nineteenth century owes not a little to Bizet, though he was regularly, and often severely, criticised for his pandering to the public taste.

Work on his statutory task as Prix de Rome scholar—a one-act opera entitled *La Guzla de L'Emir* for the Opéra Comique—engaged him for several months after his return to Paris. There were in 1860 only two theatres in Paris where the young operatic composer might hope to hear his works performed—the Opéra Comique, then under the directorship of Camille du Locle, and the Théâtre Lyrique under Carvalho. The Opéra only opened its doors to composers whose reputations were already made, thus earning for itself the nickname of *le musée de la musique*. Bizet was, of course, friendly with Gounod, whose *Faust* (1859) had given him an enormous position in the French musical world: but he must have been extremely surprised when he suddenly received in 1862 a commission from Carvalho for an opera for the Théâtre Lyrique. He was already engaged on his opera for the Opéra Comique, and it was very flattering to have both theatres competing for his favour at the age of twenty-four. *La Guzla de l'Emir* was drudgery and never appealed to Bizet; so that as soon as he received Carvalho's commission and libretto, he withdrew *La Guzla* from the Opéra Comique and concentrated entirely on the new work. Possibly he feared that the mild success, or even the possible failure, of *La Guzla* at the Opéra Comique might prejudice his chances at the Théâtre Lyrique: but he was not called upon to do as he did and burn the music which he had already written. If he was the shameless careerist which some modern critics have depicted, he would at least have put it aside for possible later use. Actually, he seems to have been conscious of its mediocrity and to have destroyed it for fear he should be tempted to have recourse to this old score when, in the future, inspiration might fail him. In January 1863 the *Scherzo*, which formed part of his third *envoi* from Rome, was given two public performances in Paris—by Pasdeloup on January 11 and a week later at the Société Nationale des Beaux Arts. Pasdeloup had founded his Concerts Populaires in 1860—cheap Sunday concerts, at which the works of Beethoven began to appear with other good foreign music (Schumann and Mendelssohn), and here and there a few French works. Bizet's *Scherzo* was hissed and several subscribers wrote to complain of the unwarranted introduction of this modern, cacophonous music into a Sunday afternoon concert! But a week later the *Scherzo* was well received and Bizet was delighted.

All his time now was devoted to the composition of Carvalho's libretto, *Les Pêcheurs de Perles*, which was produced on September 29, 1863, at the Théâtre Lyrique. The story was not a fortunate one, and the verses of MM. Carré and Cormon, the librettists, did not add to its value. The scene is laid in Ceylon, among the pearl-fishers who yearly visit the coast and camp there during the pearl-fishing season. The orchestral prelude with which the work opens is very short (43 bars), consisting merely of a 16-bar theme twice repeated, with two bars introduction and nine bars coda. The theme is fresh, supple and pleasing, innocent of any orientalism but with a certain serenity and gaiety which set the atmosphere very well for the scenery of Act I, which follows

25

immediately. The sun is beating down on a wild stretch of shore and a brilliantly blue sea, while the pearl-fishers put up their bamboo huts and tents, some still working, others dancing and drinking: all that is visible of the country inland is a ruined temple and clumps of palm trees. The open fifths of the dance on which the curtain rises and the flattened 7ths (F natural in the key of G minor) give the music the conventionally oriental flavour: but the real piquancy is supplied by the short, vigorously rhythmic phrases, starting in a low register and mounting to a climax, and the sharpened 5th (G sharp in the key of D minor) and frequent use of the intervals of the minor second. The chorus is genuinely primitive-sounding, and one of the earliest successful attempts to reproduce a ' savage ' atmosphere. A section marked *noblement*, in B flat major, follows and shatters this illusion; for the music is clearly related to Gounod and its charmingly suave harmonies carry the listener very far West of Suez. Then the dances and the original chorus are repeated until, at the unfortunate words '*dansez jusqu'au soir, dansez!* ', they suddenly break off. Zurga (baritone) solemnly invites the fishers to choose a chief, whose word they shall obey during the pearl-fishing season: and the unison chorus, once again in suave, Gounodesque phrases, elect him to rule them. He exacts an oath of absolute obedience which has hardly been taken, when a figure appears among the rocks, causing consternation among the fishers. Zurga goes forward to meet the newcomer and recognises an old friend of his youth, Nadir, who is also known to the fishers as a great huntsman.

Des savanes et des forêts
J'ai sondé l'ombre, la mystère
J'ai suivi, le poignard aux dents,
Le tigre fauve aux yeux ardents
Et le jaguar et la panthère
—he cries, and there is an air of wildness and tragedy in his voice which were prophetic, not only in the life of Nadir but also in that of Bizet.

Ex.7

cp. *Carmen*, Example 28.

Zurga and the fishermen beg Nadir to stay with them and he consents, the dances and choruses with which the act started breaking out once again, until the dancers disperse and leave Zurga and Nadir alone together. At once the atmosphere becomes tense, as Zurga asks Nadir if he has remained faithful to his oath and whether it is as a true friend that he has returned or as a traitor. Nadir answers simply and with melancholy,

' De mon amour profond j'ai su me rendre maître.'

Zurga replies with new proffers of his friendship, saying that he has banished the mad passion from his heart. Nadir answers that, though he may be calm, he will never be able to forget: and there follows the story of the two men's love for the same woman, a Brahmin priestess of Candy, seen for a moment in a temple at evening and never forgotten by either. Throughout the duet Nadir preserves a dreamlike, contemplative calm, while Zurga is more explosive and violent. A large part in suggesting the

27

rêverie is played by the orchestra, the flutes and
oboes accompanied by the strings and harp painting,
as it were, the voluptuous picture of the incense-
filled and flower-wreathed temple at sundown, while
Nadir's broken phrases fill in the details. The atmosphere changes and the story is interrupted as the
friends remember the sudden rush of jealous hatred
which overcame each for the other as they realized
their rivalry in love. But the priestess disappeared
from the temple, the friends had sworn to remain
faithful to each other, and it is in some dark way her
doing, they feel, that they have been reunited that
day. The scene, which is the key scene of the whole
opera, is most effective and must have been even
more so in 1863, when it was comparatively an
unfamiliar type. Since then Massenet's dream-scene
in *Mignon*, which owes certainly something to this
scene of Bizet's, has become famous and has
superseded the older work.

Once again a new arrival breaks in on a solemn
moment. This time it is the arrival of

Une femme inconnue et belle autant que sage

brought by deputies of the tribe to act as their
priestess during the pearl-fishing season. As she
approaches, the theme of the overture is heard
again, followed by the theme of Nadir's and
Zurga's rêverie, the whole chorus of the tribe burst

Ex.8

into a song of welcome, as they surround the woman and offer her flowers. She is heavily veiled and remains silent until Zurga solemnly addresses her, asking if she will promise to remain always veiled, to pray day and night on a rock overhanging the bay, to remain a spotless virgin and to ward off, by her songs and prayers, all evil and hostile spirits. Each question is put in slow and solemn tones, and rises through the notes of a minor third, and to each the veiled priestess answers.

The simplicity of the means and the device by which each question starts a minor third above the one before, the mystery and candour of the woman's *pianissimo* answers make the scene most moving and beautiful; and Zurga's promise of the finest pearl as a reward of her constancy, with its commonplace rhythm and melody, makes a most unhappy contrast. While Zurga and the fishermen threaten the woman with death if she breaks her word, Nadir, who has remained apart and taken no interest in the proceedings, slowly advances towards the priestess. Suddenly he starts; he has recognised her and she, at the sound of his stifled cry, recognises him. Again the theme of the rêverie is heard in the orchestra *pianissimo* and Zurga notices the trembling which seizes the woman. Suspecting that she is filled with a sudden foreboding he begs her to leave them if she cannot keep her oath; but turning towards Nadir she solemnly asserts that she will stay, whatever her fate may be. Zurga accepts her word, and after a short hymn in honour of Brahma the fishermen disperse, while the orchestra plays the theme of the prelude again.

Alone, Nadir is in an agony of remorse. He has tricked Zurga and followed the priestess of Candy, Leila, who has now come to the pearl-fishers. Zurga must know everything, must have seen and guessed the reason of his emotion, he feels; but his emotion is too much for him and he breaks into a tender and melancholy romance, after which he lies down exhausted to sleep. In the distance the voices of a chorus are just heard, punctuated by sweeping arpeggio phrases in the orchestra: and then, on a rock high above the shore, Leila appears, led by the high-priest Nourabad, who conducts her to her post and then lights a ceremonial fire on which he throws incense, bidding Leila sing as the crowd listens below. Nadir, half asleep and dreaming already of his love, murmurs ' Adieu, doux rêve' and then, above a full and gentle accompaniment in the orchestra, Leila begins her hymn. She calls on Brahma and Siva, on the spirits of the air, the water, the rocks, the meadows and woods; and the crowd murmur after her, while Nadir, roused by her voice, stands charmed on the shore. The hymn breaks off and Leila seems to sing for herself, a broken, half-sobbing song above a conventional Italian accompaniment figure. The crowd beneath are spellbound and beg her to sing on, banishing all evil spirits from the shore. Bizet probably borrowed from the *Casta diva* aria in Bellini's *Norma* the device of making the soprano sing, above a simple and harmonically conventional chorus, the trills and roulades which, whatever their musical merit, show off the singer's voice so excellently. The key is the same as Bellini's (G major), and the situation is similar. Meanwhile Nadir has crept to the foot of the rock on whose summit Leila is standing: and, as the violins change brusquely to the key of B major and play the theme of the rêverie *tremolando*, Nadir calls to her, assuring her of his presence and his willingness to die for her. For a moment she bends forward and raises the corner of her veil; and then the chorus bids her sing again, and above their subdued voices she breaks once again into the ornamental trills and arpeggios; but this time it is for Nadir she is

singing, and the act closes with his murmured
' Je suis là ', and her long drawn ' ah, ' of ecstasy.

Act II opens with a short *allegretto* in the orchestra
setting the atmosphere before the curtain rises.
The strings *pizzicato* above a soft pedal note in the
horn, a rising, half threatening passage in the
minor, and the curtain rises on the ruined temple,
a terrace above the sea and a night sky brilliant
with stars. Leila stands alone and silent, while a
chorus is heard in the distance, the basses' open
fifths throbbing like guitars and forming the
accompaniment to the women's song, only punctuated occasionally by short, glittering trills and
semi-quaver passages in the strings.

Ex. 10

blan - ches é - toi - les Se bai - gnent dans L'a-
la la la la la la la la la la la la la la la la la

-zur des flots si - len - ci - eux
la la la la la la la la la la la la la

As the voices die away Nourabad, the high priest,
advances towards Leila, telling her that the boats
are all home and she can sleep, well protected by
the sea on one hand, inaccessible cliffs on another
and an armed watch keeping guard over the only
path to the temple. She tells him that she has
already once in her life shown herself able to keep
an oath in face of death; how one evening when
she was a child a fugitive appeared at her father's
house, seeking refuge which she gave him; how his
pursuers arrived and threatened her with death,
but she would say nothing and so ensured the
fugitive's escape. He gave her a chain which she
was always to wear in memory of him; he would
never forget her service. Nourabad bids her bear
her promise in mind and think of the account
Zurga will demand of her if any misfortune befall
the fishers. He leaves her, and the orchestra hints
at the sinister and tragic events which are so close.
Then a fragment of the chorus is heard again in the
distance and, as that dies away, Leila is left alone.

There has already been a hint of the *Walküre* in
Leila's account of her rescuing the fugitive: and
now the orchestra seems to foreshadow Wagner,

only to fall back into the flattest style of Gounod,
as Leila sings how, though alone, she feels she is
guarded by Nadir. And then in the distance his
voice, heralded by a sad cry, almost like a bird's,
in the oboe. As the voice draws nearer Leila grows
more and more excited until, as Nadir appears on
the terrace, the orchestra bursts into short breathless
phrases of expectation and he takes her in his
arms. She is terrified for him and begs him to go,
but he will not listen to her, saying that the night
is young and he is safe until daybreak. He woos
her with a very banal and rather Mendelssohnian
romance: she confesses that she was waiting for
him: and they break into the inevitable unison love
duet. But Leila is still alive to their danger, and she
begs Nadir to go, promising to expect him every
evening. He leaves her; but before he has been
gone a moment there is the sound of a shot and
Nourabad's voice is heard summoning the fishermen
and calling down curses on the violation of the

sanctuary. As the tribe collects a storm gathers, the sea rises to fury and the whole chorus breaks into a lamentation—

> O nuit d'épouvante
> La mer écumante
> Soulève en grondant
> Ses flots furieux

—above a stormy semi-quaver figure in the strings. Nourabad enters, announcing that a man has been found with Leila, and he leads forward the two culprits. The tribe is horror struck at first and then bursts into violent hatred and imprecation, demanding the death of both Leila and Nadir. Here Bizet has almost equalled the Gluck of *Iphigénie en Tauride* in the dramatic violence and explosiveness of his music—

Ex. 12

rising to the almost hysterical hatred of

Ex. 13

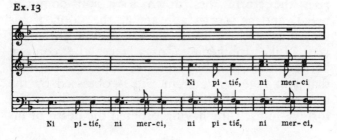

35

Ni pi - tié, ni mer - ci Pour eux la mort!

ni pi - tié, ni mer - ci Pour eux la mort!

ni pi - tié, ni mer - ci Pour eux la mort!

Zurga finally manages to calm the crowd and
exert his authority: the culprits are to go un-
punished on the condition that they go at once.
Nourabad, however, demands that Leila remove
her veil and make her shame known to all before
she leaves. He seizes her veil roughly, and there
stands before him the priestess of Candy. In a
moment he is mad with fury and calls on the
fishermen to avenge themselves and him, and the
fierce chorus breaks out again, demanding death
and not mercy, till the act finishes with the solemn
hymn to Brahma, swearing to avenge the sacrilege.
At the beginning of Act III, before the curtain
goes up, the storm is raging in the orchestra,
with all the conventional diminished sevenths and
chromatic scales of the nineteenth century's operatic
thunder and lightning. Just before the curtain
rises the storm dies down to a soft dominant
pedal, and as Zurga appears at the door of his
tent it is nothing more than a distant chromatic
wail. Like Iphigénie, Zurga feels the contrast
between the calming of the storm and the passions
that still rage within him. He is obsessed by the
thought of Nadir and his treachery: but he cannot
forgive himself for having ordered the death of his

best friend and he breaks into a tender and emotional appeal to their old friendship, rejecting what has happened as a horrible nightmare. As he sinks overcome with remorse, and his broken sobs are heard in the orchestra, Leila appears, and once again the theme of the rêverie is heard in the orchestra. Hesitantly she comes forward and in her voice are all the accents of pleading and desperation. Zurga feels that it is a god who has sent her to punish him with her beauty, greater now, when she is about to die, than ever before. He tells her not to be afraid but to speak. Then with all the passion of which she is capable she begs for pardon, not for herself but for the innocent Nadir. Her voice is broken with emotion and she can only speak in short sobbing phrases. Finally she brings forward her last plea: Nadir's freedom will make her own death more easy. This is too much for Zurga and his jealousy breaks through all control. He might have pardoned Nadir, his friend: but Leila's very plea of her love for him has damned him irrevocably—

Son crime est d'être aimé quand je ne le suis pas

Three times, her voice rising at each plea, Leila begs to be allowed to bear all the brunt of Zurga's jealous fury: then at last she loses patience and bursts into a final desperate cry—

> Va, prends aussi ma vie:
> Mais, ta rage assouvie,
> Le remords, l'infâmie
> Te poursuivront toujours

—above a vigorous, typically Verdian rhythm, ♪ ♫♫ , ♫ ♫ and the scene ends with her solemn malediction of Zurga. In the distance can be heard the sounds of dancing and singing, the preparations for the ghastly sacrifice which is to take place at dawn. Leila suddenly becomes calm and, as the rêverie theme appears in the orchestra, she turns to Zurga and hands him a necklace which she asks to be given to her mother when she is dead. With a wild cry in the orchestra the scene closes and the curtain falls.

The final scene is a deserted spot on the coast and as the curtain rises the fishermen are discovered dancing and drinking in preparation for the sacrifice. In contrast with the dances of joy with which the opera opened, these have a sombre, almost brutal character, made wilder by the cries of the women to Brahma, high above the muttered threats of the men. Then Leila and Nadir are led in solemn procession on to the stage—and here Bizet made use of the *Marche funèbre* of his last *envoi* from Rome—while Nourabad leads the fishermen in a prayer to the dark gods to whom the culprits are being sacrificed. A faint glow touches the sky and, crying on the dawn, two priests lift their daggers over Leila and Nadir, when Zurga rushes on to the stage. It is not the dawn, but a vast fire in the fishermen's camp which is lighting the sky: and the crowd rushes to save children and possessions, their thoughts all on their own safety and quite forgetting the sacrifice. Only Nourabad has his suspicions, and while Zurga is left alone with Leila and Nadir, he hides behind a rock. Zurga explains that he has started the fire in the camp; he cuts the ropes that bind Nadir and, turning to Leila and showing her the necklace she entrusted to him, he bids her be free, as she once freed him in her childhood. Nourabad runs to warn the fishermen; and the lovers burst into a hymn of gratitude and happiness, joined in an ecstasy of resignation by Zurga. But they have only just time to escape as the fishermen come running back to avenge themselves. Zurga is stabbed as he prevents them following the lovers: and as he lies dying on the shore, the rêverie theme appears for the last time in the orchestra and is taken up by the lovers as they stand on a rock high above the stage, on their way to freedom and safety.

Les Pêcheurs de Perles was not a brilliantly original libretto; but it had one characteristic which recommended it to Bizet and called out in him a quality which was to remain his greatest asset. An exotic setting—whether it be the East, or Scotland, or Spain—was a challenge to Bizet's sense of atmosphere. We have seen him in his letters enchanted with Italy; and although he never left France again in the flesh, he was a tireless traveller in the spirit. Ferdinand David had set the fashion for the oriental in music, with his *Désert* (1844) and *Lalla Roukh* (1862): and there were several critics who traced his influence in *Les Pêcheurs de Perles*. But in reality the oriental tradition was far older and forms a steady stream in the history of French art— —from the *Lettres persanes* of Montesquieu (1721) through the chinoiseries of the eighteenth century to the *Orientales* of Victor Hugo, the oriental pictures of Delacroix, and in music F. David, Bizet and later Delibes (*Lakmé*) and Reyer (*Salammbô*). Berlioz, in the *Journal des Débats*, recognised the germ of genius in *Les Pêcheurs* and found 'a considerable number of fine, expressive passages, full of fire and richly coloured '. There were the inevitable critics who discovered a Wagnerian influence, though Bizet had probably heard none of Wagner's music when he composed the score; but the epithet Wagnerian was merely a term of abuse in the Paris of 1863 and was apt to be used for any new or originally conceived work, any harmonic daring and any deviation from the flattest and most conventional melody. The real danger to Bizet which is clear in the score of *Les Pêcheurs* is the undigested influence of Gounod. Apropos of *Les Pêcheurs*, Gounod wrote to Bizet— ' Be very much *yourself:* that is the way to stand quite alone to-day but to have a crowd round you in the future '. It was the best advice that he could give: but nine years later Gounod was writing again to Bizet from London—'. . . you tell me that you have felt anxiety caused by the fear of being absorbed: such a feeling in you, and on my account has caused me profound astonishment '. But Bizet was right. He felt very strongly the attraction of Gounod's bland emotion: and, under-developed himself on the emotional side, he tended—and most notably in *Les Pêcheurs*—to fall back on Gounod in any scene where the expression of tender emotion was asked of him. The love duet between Leila and Nadir in Act II and the final trio between Leila, Nadir and Zurga bear witness to this: and the whole character of Leila is fundamentally unoriginal in conception. The most original and most promising features are the treatment of the chorus and orchestra, and the character of Zurga. Bizet's contempt for women and for love—an adolescent phase, as the tone

40

of the letters in which he expresses it shows—
stood him in bad stead when he came to write any
more serious love-music than the philanderings of
Don Procopio. The moments of real originality in
Les Pêcheurs are flashes: as in so many first works,
the flashes of genius tend to be hidden behind
clouds of mere talent. The eleven bars in the
orchestra, for instance, which mark Zurga's exit
at the end of Act II, Scene 1,

Ex. 14

are sandwiched between long passages of an excellent pupil's talent: but they contain a dramatic vividness, a boldness and a tragic sense from which an acute critic such as Berlioz could foretell something of the vividness and tragedy of *Carmen*.

CHAPTER III

THE reception of the *Pêcheurs de Perles* had been encouraging and Bizet must have felt that he had laid the foundations at least of a brilliant future. But the present was pressing and, most pressing of all, his need for ready money. Although he had been well paid for the *Pêcheurs de Perles* he must have some regular source of income, and he was obliged to undertake for publishers ,work which was pure drudgery and merely interrupted his own serious composition—orchestration of dance music, reduction of full scores to piano versions, and the making of various vocal anthologies such as were popular with our grandparents. His letters and the reminiscences of his friends show him working often into the small hours, taking no rest and undermining a constitution which had never been robust. In Rome he had found it difficult to make up his mind on the real position of Verdi: this indecision was now replaced by a fanatical admiration. In his spare time he set to work on a new opera, *Ivan le Terrible,* which was to be composed entirely in Verdi's manner: and not content with this, he determined to try and remedy the one-sidedness of his education and to acquire some of that general information and culture which his concentration upon music—and, it should be added, his natural inclination—had caused him to neglect. He was encouraged in his reading by a pupil, Edmond Galabert, who had written to him after the success of *Pêcheurs de Perles* and asked Bizet to give him lessons. Galabert was an amateur and his circumstances did not allow him to live in Paris, but Bizet, attracted by his letters and his obvious enthusiasm and talent for music, consented to give him a ' correspondence class ', refusing all payment. Some of his letters to Galabert throw light on his own character and conception of music. In the summer of 1865 he writes, laughing affectionately at the rather stiff and cold manner of some of Galabert's work:

'Go on, try to achieve real pathos, avoid dryness, and don't be too afraid of sensuous beauty, you austere philosopher. Think of Mozart and study him unceasingly. Provide yourself with *Don Giovanni, Figaro,* the *Magic Flute* and *Così fan tutte.* Look at Weber too. Long live sunshine and love!'

Mozart was the deepest and most constant admiration of Bizet's life: and it is interesting to see that, even at the height of his own enthusiasm for Verdi, it is to Mozart and Weber that he refers his pupil. Galabert, though, was more than a pupil and Bizet could unburden himself and air his opinions on life in general to him. In October 1866, in answer to a letter from Galabert on the subject of religion, Bizet wrote something like a confession of faith:

'I perfectly understand what you say about religion. I agree with you too: but do not let us be unjust. We agree on a principle which can be formulated thus, I think. "Religion is a means of exploitation employed by the strong against the weak; religion is the cloak of ambition,

44

injustice and vice ". The progress of which you speak is slow but sure; by degrees it destroys all superstitions. Truth is extricating itself, science is being popularised, religion is shaken and will fall soon—in a few centuries, that is to say to-morrow. That will be excellent: but do not let us forget that religion, with which you and I and a few others can now dispense, has itself been an admirable instrument of progress: it is religion, and especially Catholicism, which has taught us the precepts which enable us to-day to dispense with her. Like thankless children we turn and rend the breast which has fed us, because the food which it now gives is now no longer worthy of us: we despise this false illumination, which has for all that gradually accustomed our eyes to the light. Without it we should have been blind from the cradle, for ever. . . . Do you think that an admirable impostor like Moses did not make a great step forward in philosophy—and so for humanity? Look at that sublime absurdity which we call the Bible! Is it not possible to extract from this magnificent gallimaufry most of the truths which we know to-day? At that time they had to be clothed in the dress of the age, they had to wear the livery of error, lies, imposture. Dogma and religion have had a definitely happy influence on mankind. If you quote the persecutions, crimes and infamies perpetrated in their name, I reply that humanity burned its fingers at the torch. Millions of men massacred by their fellows, a drop in the ocean, nothing! . . . . Mankind is not yet strong enough to amputate faith. Sad, but what can we do? Religion is a policeman. Later we shall do without policemen, and judges too. We have already made a great step forward, since this policeman hardly suffices for us. Ask society which it prefers to give up, bishops or policemen . . . and you will see what a vast majority is in favour of the policeman! The law is strong enough nowadays to restrain evil passions. Law would have had no effect on the Hebrews, who had no idea of philosophy. They had to have altars, Sinais with Véry lights, etc. An appeal had to be made to their eyes: later an appeal to their imaginations was enough. At present our only appeal is to reason. I believe that all the future belongs to various perfectings of our social contract (with which politics are always concerning themselves, so foolishly!). A perfect society means no more injustice and therefore no more attacks on the social contract, no more priests, no more policemen, no more crimes, no more adulteries, no more prostitution, no more strong feelings, no more passions. One moment . . . no more music, no more poetry, no legion of honour, no press (that's one good thing), no theatre at all, no error, and so—no art! The devil take it, but it's your fault. Your inevitable, implacable progress kills art, poor art!. The societies most riddled with superstition have been the great promoters of art: Egypt, architecture: Greece, the plastic arts: the Renaissance, Raphael, Phidias, Mozart, Beethoven, Veronese, Weber—madmen all of them! The fantastic, hell, paradise, djinns, phantoms, ghosts, fairies—that is the realm of art. Only prove to me that we should have an art of reason, truth and exactitude, and I pass into your camp, bag and baggage. . . . As a musician I declare that if you suppress adultery, fanaticism, crime, error, the supernatural, it is impossible to write a single note more. Art has its own philosophy, though one has to twist the sense of words a bit to define it . . . the *science of wisdom* . . . yes, except that it is exactly the opposite. Look here, I am a miserable philosopher as you see: well, I can promise you that I should write better music if I believed a lot of things which are not true! Let us sum up: art retreats as reason advances. You don't believe it, but it is true. Make me a Dante or a Homer nowadays. Out of what? The imagination lives on chimeras and visions. Suppress the chimeras and good-bye to the imagination. No more art, science everywhere. If you say "what is the harm in that?", I give up and argue no more, *because you are right*. Nevertheless it is a pity, a great pity . . . literature will escape through philosophy. We shall have Voltaires. That is a consolation, but we shall have Jean-Jacques too, because you will never change the stuff of which men are made; and I have a horror of this medley of vice, sentimentality, philosophy, and genius which produced Rousseau. The three-headed calf . . . the three-faced man. Ugh! let's leave him. An hysterical, cynical hypocrite, republican and sensitive to finish the picture! Georges Sand imitates him, a terrible punishment.'

Bizet was a child of his time: but his anti-clericalism and his pathetic expression of faith in science must not be mistaken for a real hostility to religion. As the second part of his letter shows, he was too much of an artist—too firm a believer in the mysteriousness of the greatest things in the world— to be an atheist: and like the Voltaire of whom he wrote from Rome so admiringly, it is the church that he attacks rather than religion, although like Voltaire he does not always manage to keep the distinction clear in his writing. He longed for the faith of a romantic and felt in duty bound to admire the achievements of science. His certainty of the clear distinction between truth and falsehood (' I should write better music if I believed a lot of things which are not true ') was typical of his generation, for whom it was difficult to realise that beliefs which could, as Bizet himself felt, fertilise and set in action the deepest and noblest creative powers must, for that very reason, have a great proportion of truth in them. Science, then at her most cocksure and aggressive, persuaded a whole generation that she was infallible and that they should have none other gods but her: and Bizet was clever and alive enough to see the strength of her claims, but neither intellectually nor morally profound enough to realise their excessiveness. He was, as he says, no philosopher and on the whole he bothered his head very little with abstract questions, living by his emotions and that natural sense and gift for life which is one of the greatest and most endearing qualities of the French.

Meanwhile his opera *Ivan le Terrible* was finished and had been accepted by the Théâtre Lyrique, when Bizet suddenly thought better of it, withdrew his score and burnt it. There is no adequate

explanation of his action except his artist's conscience: for at the moment he had no other work
on hand, as he had when he withdrew the *Guzla
de l'Emir* in favour of the *Pêcheurs de Perles*. Most
of the score has been preserved in a rather sketchy
and imperfect condition, and from this it is evident
that Bizet did right. *Ivan le Terrible* was not a
worthy successor to the *Pêcheurs de Perles*: the
story was weak and the music thoroughly derivative.
But it was worth writing if only because it finally
exorcised the ghost of Verdi from Bizet's musical
consciousness. Indeed the ghost was exorcised
almost too thoroughly, for two years later (March
1867) we find him writing to Edmond Galabert

'I have just come from [the first performance of]
Don Carlos. It is *very bad*. You know that I am
eclectic; I adore *Traviata* and *Rigoletto*. *Don
Carlos* is a kind of compromise. No melody, no
[dramatic] accent: there is an attempt at a style,
but it is no more than an attempt.'

'Wagner, c'est Verdi avec du style' is a remark
that used to be attributed, though quite apocryphally,
to Bizet. His remark about *Don Carlos* seems to
be the nearest approach to it. It would be interesting
to know what Bizet meant by the 'style' which he
finds unsuccessfully attempted by Verdi in *Don
Carlos*. Verdi was of course writing for the Paris
Opera when he wrote *Don Carlos*, and he was
certainly influenced by the works of Meyerbeer,
which were still the patterns of French 'grand'
opera. Meyerbeer, as we have seen, was not one
of Bizet's favourites, although he did not always
escape his influence: and 'style' in this context
may mean the style of Meyerbeer. But Bizet was

inclined sometimes to use terms of musical criticism rather vaguely. From Rome he had written (page 12) of the *motif*, that one necessity for a musician's (financial) salvation, without making it clear exactly what he meant by the word. He was probably, in the case of *Don Carlos,* doing little more than trying to explain or, in the psychologist's phrase, to ' rationalise ' an instinctive dislike of the latest work of a composer whom he felt he had outgrown.

Meanwhile he had received from the Théâtre Lyrique another commission for an opera based, this time, on Sir Walter Scott's *Fair Maid of Perth.* He was living outside Paris during 1866 at Le Vésinet, where he found it easier to devote himself entirely to his work. The orchestrations and arrangements—all the drudgery of a publisher's hack, in fact—still took up a great deal of his time: and it is astonishing to find him, in addition to this and his work on the new opera, beginning a symphonic poem *Roma (Souvenirs de Rome)* and six short songs, *Feuilles d'Album.* The songs, it is true, are completely worthless musically and little more than a frank supply in answer to the demand for easy and sentimental drawing-room melodies. The poems are for the most part worthless, the prosody is appalling (*de* and *le* often bearing the strong accent of the bar) and the music quite without individuality. *Roma* is a very different work. A symphonic poem of quite conventional form, it nevertheless shows Bizet as a serious orchestral composer. The first movement, which was afterwards entitled *La Chasse dans la Forêt d'Ostie,* opens with an *Andante tranquillo,* a full theme in the brass only, which Bizet has marked *piano mais sonore*. Gradually the wood-wind and the strings are brought in and in the short coda to this section a harp effect is introduced (*sons harmoniques, aussi marqués que possible*). This is succeeded by a piece of conventional storm-music, with diminished sevenths and semi-quaver triplets, rising in speed to the *Allegro agitato*. The strings in unison announce the new theme, accompanied by double-basses *pizzicato* and a tensely rhythmical phrase in the wood-wind. As the phrases of the theme are tossed from strings to horns and jets of wood-wind thirds break in like flashes of lightning, the music rises to a climax and above the storm the clarinet announces a beautifully simple phrase, in 2-2 time against the surging 6-8 of the rest of the orchestra, interrupted again and again but returning with more and more insistence in the strings, until it is finally drowned by the storm. A sudden lull, and a distant horn call re-introduces the theme of the opening *Andante tranquillo* against the mutterings of the storm: but once again the storm rises and drowns it. At last, though, the storm dies away and the movement ends with a shortened reprise of the opening *Andante* and a short coda. The *Allegro vivace* (the Scherzo which Bizet wrote in Rome) in A flat major opens with a fugato in the strings, one phrase of which is developed for some time and leads to a more serious theme in the strings accompanied by a running figure in the wood-wind. There is much play with enharmonic modulations (See Ex. 15) and the Trio continues the atmosphere of the D flat major theme against hints of the opening fugato. The whole movement owes

Ex. 15

something to Weber, for whom Bizet had a great admiration, and especially to the Scherzo of the piano sonata in A flat. The slow movement (*Andante molto*) which follows is in F major and consists of two main themes (A and B), in the scheme A B B A: neither is of great melodic value and both hail from the world of Gounodesque religiosity. It is emphatically the weakest movement of the work, though Bizet himself felt that the last movement was not up to the rest. This last movement is a Tarantella and was given the name of Carnival. It is in C minor and opens with a succession of chords based on two diminished sevenths which act as a kind of ostinato throughout much of the movement. A gay theme in the relative major appears at first in the strings, and then in the full orchestra, introducing the carnival procession,

Ex. 16

which clashes with the religious element typified by the second theme (B) of the slow movement. The two processions interrupt one another, a phrase of the one bursting in on a phrase of the other, until the two seem inextricably mixed, the religious theme appearing in the brass and wood-wind set against a long trill in the strings and leading to a recapitulation and coda.

Bizet's whole conception of Rome appears in this score. The dominant impression is contrast— the Rome of the Popes and all the splendour of the Church set against nature and the countryside (first movement) and against the mundane gaiety and frivolity of an Italian city (last movement). The two middle movements show these two elements more undiluted, mundane gaiety dominating the Scherzo and the more serious, religious element dominating the slow movement. The orchestration is brilliant and though the ideas are not always original, both Gounod and Weber counting for a good deal, as we have seen, the whole work is thoroughly alive and well above the standard of the time for such orchestral suites. *Roma* was not performed until February 1869, when it was given by Pasdeloup at the Cirque Napoléon without the Scherzo. The score was not printed until after Bizet's death, when all four movements were brought together under the title of *Roma*.

Meanwhile he worked on his commission from the Théâtre Lyrique and even on one occasion entered the ranks of the critics. This was in August 1867, when he wrote an article in the newly-founded Révue Nationale under the name of Gaston de Betzi. It was Bizet's first appearance as a writer, as he told his readers, warning them, in a witty disclaimer, not to expect literary excellence. It is a violent and forceful article, obviously sincere, in defence of a liberal and generous attitude towards music, and in protest against the labels of school and nationality which critics have always loved. 'For me', he says, echoing Rossini, 'there are only two kinds of music—good and bad.' He protests against amateurishness on the one hand and pedantry on the other: and sets up a vigorous, common sense, yet high-minded, ideal of musical criticism. It is a pity that it was his one incursion into journalism: his verve and generosity would have been welcome in the name-calling and carping world of contemporary musical criticism, from which he had already suffered himself and was to suffer again.

The poem of the *Jolie Fille de Perth* was the fruit of a collaboration between Saint Georges and Adenis. If anything it is worse than the libretto of *Pêcheurs de Perles*. Sir Walter Scott's Scots are transformed into the bastard Italians of Donizetti's *Lucia di Lammermoor*, and nothing but the truncated skeleton of the story of the Fair Maid of Perth is left. The Prelude sets the tone of the music of the whole work—preponderantly Italian, with its passages in sixths and thirds, the facile melody over the simple rocking accompaniment, and the final *cabaletta* which recall Bellini and Donizetti rather than Verdi. The curtain rises on the workshop of Armourer Smith, the anvils sounding in the orchestra and the workmen joining in a conventional chorus, *bien rhythmé*. Smith announces the celebration of carnival beginning that evening, the holiday from work and the search for pleasure: his workmen take up his words and leave the workshop singing to the same polonaise rhythm as that of the opening chorus. Left alone, Smith is just embarking on sentimental reflections on his coming marriage, when he is interrupted by the noise of a scuffle in the street, the door of the shop bursts open and Mab, the gipsy, stumbles in asking for protection against the pressing attentions of a band of *jeunes seigneurs*. She soon recovers herself, admitting that she was ready to give them the kisses they wanted but not prepared to have them stolen from her: in her gratitude to Smith she offers to read his hand, while in the orchestra there appears the first hint of another and more formidable gipsy who was to concern Bizet later—

Ex. 17

She announces that Smith's fiancée, Catherine, and her father, Simon Glover, are coming to dinner with him, and at that moment there is a knock at the door and Mab is hustled into a neighbouring room for fear of her presence exciting Catherine's jealousy. Smith's guests enter with the news that carnival is already beginning, which they announce in a charming trio, Catherine and her father being joined by Ralph, Glover's apprentice. Smith receives them to an elegant Italian figure in the orchestra: but he is cut short by Glover's pre-occupation with the dinner which he has brought and the *vieux Wisky d'Ecosse*. The apprentice is jealous of Smith and tries to interrupt his conversation with Catherine: but she barely notices either, being taken up with the thrill of the carnival, *les plaisirs et les fleurs,* and breaking into a brilliant coloratura aria, with a gay polonaise accompaniment. Glover becomes impatient for his dinner and moves towards the kitchen, calling Ralph to follow him: but Ralph is most unwilling to leave Catherine alone with Smith, and when he finally obeys his master, it is only with a cry of ' war to the death ' hurled at Smith. The love-making scene which follows is a great improvement on scenes of the same kind in *Pêcheurs de Perles*. Smith's timid advances and Catherine's rather coquettish holding back are woven together by a strong, almost independent orchestral accompaniment which shows Bizet, although very much under Italian influence, yet learning to construct an independent scene, with good characterisation and a vital orchestral part, an expressive melody and, despite the critics of the day, some successful ornamentation which becomes the flirtatious Catherine very well. The lovers are interrupted, just as Smith has given Catherine a small jewelled flower, by the entrance of an elegant · stranger, who asks to have his dagger-blade made good. His words give an unpleasant hint of both his character and station— ' I have blunted my blade in some yokel's arm: give it your attention ' (*Ma dague s'est faussée dans le bras d'un manant. Soignez donc la blessée*). Smith dislikes and distrusts the stranger, Catherine finds him insolent but attractive and declares that through him she can give the jealous Smith a lesson. The stranger is the Duke of Rothsay, governor of Perth, and he sets himself at once to make a conquest of Catherine. All this in a trio very skilfully constructed, without any great characterisation of the parts but with a Schumannesque charm and simplicity that is in itself very pleasant.

While the Duke flirts with Catherine, Smith works on the dagger blade and contrives to make so much noise that he drowns the compliments which he thinks are being received too favourably by Catherine. Refusing his name, the Duke invites Catherine to a ball at the palace that night (it is strange that it did not occur to her that it was probably the Duke if he invited her to the palace). Smith cannot catch exactly what they are saying, but when the stranger takes Catherine's hand, in spite of her protestations, and kisses it ardently, he turns in real fury, hammer in hand, and is only prevented from attacking the intruder by Mab, who rushes from the neighbouring room and separates them. The quartet which follows, holding up the action in the traditional Italian manner, is purely Italian too in its musical inspiration and is more creditable to Bizet's imitative than to his inventive faculties. So soon as the dramatic tension expressed in the quartet is released, Catherine breaks out into frank fury and, as jealous now as Smith had been of the stranger, demands what Mab is doing in Smith's house. She will not let him explain and insists on leaving at once, when a tipsy song is heard and her father and his apprentice enter, well primed with the *vieux Wisky d'Ecosse*. Glover immediately recognises the Duke, who has thoroughly enjoyed the lovers' quarrel and now leaves the party *en famille*, as he says, accompanied by the same elegant and flighty phrase as marked his first entry.

Ex. 18

The dispute continues, Catherine throwing away the flower Smith has given her, Glover pooh-poohing Catherine's suspicions, and the act ends in a quintet, Glover and Ralph trolling their tipsy song, while Catherine and Smith are at their several wits' ends, and Mab (who has picked up the rose) commenting benevolently on the imbroglio her intervention has caused.

Act II opens with the night-patrol going their rounds in the town of Perth, an orchestral march followed by a pianissimo chorus assuring all good citizens that they can sleep in peace. No sooner have the patrol gone, however, than the carnival chorus bursts on to the scene, led by the duke, who abdicates his rank for the night and proclaims himself and his people the subjects of *la folie*. The drinking contest which he inaugurates leads to the conventional drinking chorus, with innumerable repetitions of *oui, buvons, mes amis*—

a flat and perfunctory movement in C major but de rigueur in the French lyric theatre of the day. When Mab enters with her gipsies the music becomes alive: and the *Danse Bohémienne* is the highest point of Bizet's achievement hitherto— an ostinato figure revolving round the dominant F sharp, with arabesques above and working to a frenzied climax and wild shouts as the dancers spin round madly and finally end, with a howl and a leap, at the Duke's feet. Here Bizet caught, as never more effectively, the exotic atmosphere, without technical knowledge of primitive and non-European music, but with the intuitive understanding and grasp of the technical peculiarities that only an artist of real merit can possess.

After the dance the Duke leads Mab aside and confides in her his designs on Catherine. He is so amorous and, considering the fact that Mab herself is one of his old flames, so indiscreet that she twits him with it, in one of those sinister gipsy phrases that Bizet understood, somehow, so well.

Ex. 19

Once again a conventionally coquettish song of Mab's lets down the standard of the music, its staccato sixths and thirds, dotted semi-quavers and portamento intervals giving the lie to the gipsy harshness of the example above. However, Mab consents to smuggle Catherine, masked and in a litter, to the palace that very evening—though she makes some mental reservations of her own as she promises. The carnival chorus returns with its banal gaiety and the Duke and Mab are lost in the crowd, which itself disperses and leaves only the melancholy lover Smith. He is in despair at Catherine's anger and tries a serenade, though he is sceptical of its success. Here Bizet made use of one of the most successful numbers of *Don Procopio,* a conventional Italian air with a guitar accompaniment in 6-8 time—no better and no worse than hundreds of others of the same kind, but hopelessly out of place in the market-place of Perth. As midnight strikes and he sees no light at Catherine's window, he consoles himself with the hope of better luck tomorrow, and goes home. His place is taken by his rival, the apprentice Ralph, who has drowned his disappointment in whisky and rails against love and against womankind in between the snatches of muzzy song. Finally he is overcome with sleep and drops on a bench outside Smith's window.

The duke's majordomo, who appears on the scene looking for Catherine, can get nothing out of him. A masked woman appears from Catherine's door, enters the duke's litter and moves off towards the castle. This strikes even Ralph's sozzled brain, and after collecting himself for a moment he beats on Smith's door and shouts to him that Catherine has been taken away by the duke's men. Smith rushes off in pursuit, leaving Ralph thunderstruck in the street, while Catherine appears at her window, humming the theme of Smith's serenade. Ralph thinking he sees an apparition and that the real Catherine must have disappeared to the castle, falls to his knees as the act closes.

Act III opens with a long orchestral minuet, played with the curtain up and disclosing a room giving on to the ballroom in the castle. The minuet is in the nature of an entr'acte and points forward clearly to the famous harp and flute entr'acte which precedes the third act of *Carmen*. The key and the simple broken arpeggio accompaniment figure are both the same: but here the atmosphere is one of elegance and a distinctly eighteenth century grace. The opening scene of the act, which follows immediately, shows the Duke and his courtiers in a gaming room off the ballroom. The music recalls the ballroom scenes in Verdi's *Ballo in maschera*, which Bizet must have known, and it is effective in its light frivolity. The Duke tells his friends of the beauty he is expecting, elaborating his fatuous passion in a banal Italian air. As the veiled woman enters, the theme of his love-making with Catherine is heard in the orchestra. The Duke leads her forward and asks her to unmask. She refuses and the Duke dismisses his friends with the professional Don Juan's leer: the two are left alone. The masked woman is of course Mab, the gipsy, who wishes to have her own revenge on the Duke and at the same time to help her friend Catherine. The minuet of the entr'acte is now played again, and forms the background to the Duke's conversation with Mab. He begs her to take off her mask, telling her that he has never loved any woman as he loves her. Mab smiles sourly to herself, but she allows him to take the enamelled rose dropped by Catherine during her quarrel with Smith. When the Duke finally tries to embrace her she eludes him and runs from the room. As he pursues her, leaving the stage empty, the last elegant phrases of the minuet sound, with a cynical complacency, in the orchestra. Now Smith appears, dishevelled and at his wits' end, alternately abusing and cajoling Catherine to himself and finally, in conventional despair, calling on death. As the Duke and his courtiers appear again he hides himself, and to his amazement sees Catherine and her father presented to the Duke. Glover comes to announce his daughter's engagement to Smith. The Duke, who thinks that he has only a few moments before parted from Catherine, is amazed at her self-possession and also at her cynicism. He says quizzically that he thought she had quarrelled with Smith and Catherine answers simply that it was a passing cloud and she has determined to make things up. Smith then comes out of his hiding-place, trembling with rage, and publicly accuses

Catherine of having spent the night in the palace with the Duke. She turns to the Duke to refute Smith's accusation, but he merely comforts her, saying that her secret shall die with him. Catherine is completely bewildered, for only her father still believes in her innocence. The crowd of courtiers hardly know what to believe, touched by her beauty and apparent innocence, yet unable to dismiss the circumstantial evidence. After a full and dramatic chorus, Catherine plays her last card and appeals to Smith's love and his knowledge of her, in a touching prayer for his confidence. This leads to the final chorus which closes the act.

Here Bizet shows a new power of characterisation and an ability to build up a large and dramatic choral scene, in the Italian manner certainly but with a confidence, a breadth of melody and an interest and movement in the part-writing which he had not achieved hitherto. Smith is convinced and prepared to forgive, or to believe, Catherine until he sees the Duke wearing the enamelled flower which he gave to her the day before: once again his love turns to loathing, and the act ends with disaster.

Act IV takes place on St. Valentine's day. The curtain goes up on Smith seated, with his head in his hands, in front of his shop. Ralph and a crowd of Glover's workmen come up to him and ask him to reconsider his judgement of Catherine, of whose innocence they are all convinced. Smith hardly listens to them and finally Ralph calls him a liar and invites him to appeal to the judgement of God, in a single combat. Left alone, Smith regrets that it is not the Duke whom he is to fight.

Catherine joins him, and at the sound of her voice his anger melts and together they indulge in sentimental regrets of their lost youth and love, Smith still refusing to believe in her innocence, but apparently more from vanity than conviction. The trumpet-signal for the duel interrupts them and he leaves her, assuring her that her honour will be vindicated and he will die. At this Catherine faints and is taken into her house by Glover. The Valentine's Day chorus which follows owes a considerable amount to the opening chorus of Gounod's *Mireille*, though it has not the same charm and freshness. Mab now arrives to say that the duel has been prevented by the arrival of the Duke, to whom she has explained everything. But it is too late: Catherine has gone out of her mind. She appears and sings some fatuous roulades and arpeggios which were the conventional symbol for nineteenth century operatic madness, whether it be Lucia or Ophelia. Smith's appearance, however, recovers her and his serenade, which had such little success before, this time restores her reason, the act ending with the Valentine chorus.

La Jolie Fille de Perth is an unequal work, tailing off badly in the last act, and the general standard of the music is low. It often looks as though Bizet were going to become little more than a skilful writer of conventional Franco-Italian opera, his individuality swamped in the blend of Verdi, Gounod and Meyerbeer which he conceived to be the public taste. Admittedly, the poem might dull the inspiration of the most gifted composer, and no doubt accounts for many of the weak moments in Bizet's score.

Apart from a few touches of originality, the *Jolie Fille de Perth* has very little objective worth. Its real value lay in the exercise in dramatic writing, and particularly in the writing of choral ensembles, which it meant for Bizet. He was not really interested in the story, perhaps; and none of the protagonists appealed to him. Mab is the nearest approach to successful characterisation and the gipsy touch, which was to fascinate him later, already called out more from him than did the conventional operatic figures of the Duke, Catherine, and Smith. While he was working on the score he wrote enthusiastically to Galabert.

' The orchestra gives my whole music a colour and a relief which I dared not hope for, I confess. . . . I am holding my own. Now, forward! One must rise, rise, rise and go on rising. No more parties, no more games, no more mistresses: that's all finished and done with. I am serious. I have met an adorable girl, whom I worship. In two years' time she will be my wife. Between now and then nothing but work, reading; thought is the very stuff of life (*penser, c'est vivre*). I am serious, quite convinced and sure of myself. The good has triumphed over the evil, the victory is won!'

The girl was Geneviève Halévy, daughter of his old master at the Conservatoire, whom Bizet married in July 1869. His enthusiasm is touching and very natural: but another letter, written to his friend Paul Lacombe three months before, throws more light on to Bizet's character as a musician and especially during the composition of the *Jolie Fille de Perth*.

' I lived three years in Italy and moulded myself not on the shameful musical ways of the country but on the temperament of one or two of her composers. My senses are enthralled by Italian music—facile, idle, amorous, lascivious and passionate all at once. By conviction, at heart, and in my soul I am German . . . but I sometimes get lost in houses of musical ill fame. And, I confess to you beneath my breath, I love it when I do.'

This is perhaps the real conflict which always troubled Bizet. His affinity with Italian music is plain enough: but hitherto the side of his nature which he calls German had been satisfied with the music of Gounod, which often inspired him, and was to inspire him to the end, when he wished to depict simple goodness or unsensual love. The critics abused the *Jolie Fille de Perth* from both sides, the reactionaries producing their usual cry of ' Wagnerism,' and the more progressive, like Reyer, finding fault with the roulades and fioriture in the part of Catherine. Bizet naturally ignored the first: but he was conscious of having been too complaisant towards Devries, who took the part of Catherine, and he wrote personally to Reyer, accusing himself and promising to be more scrupulous in the future. In actual fact Catherine's roulades are harmless and not always inept, and the ' complaisance ' in the *Jolie Fille de Perth* is more deep-seated. After *Les Pêcheurs de Perles* the *Jolie Fille* was a retrogression: the promise of the earlier work is not fulfilled and it seems as if the days of ceaseless hackwork had blunted Bizet's originality. Now more than at any other time he was in danger of a fatal compromise with the demands of commercial music. Perhaps nothing less than the revolution in his private life caused by his marriage, and the national disaster of the Franco-Prussian War could shake him out of the dull acquiescence into which he was threatening to sink.

CHAPTER IV

THE reception of *La Jolie Fille de Perth* had not been satisfactory enough to make any noticeable change in Bizet's financial position, and he was still forced to take from music publishers almost any work they might choose to give him. His engagement to Geneviève Halévy may have given him more self-confidence: but, as he says in his letter to Galabert in October 1867, it also determined him to work even harder, and too hard for his health. 'From now until my marriage', he wrote, 'nothing but work and reading: *penser, c'est vivre.*' And he spent the eighteen months between the production of the *Jolie Fille de Perth* (December 26, 1867) and his marriage in June 1869 working not only at arrangements and composition, but also trying once again to cultivate and, as he saw it, to ' modernise ' himself. In August 1868 he wrote to Galabert:

'For the last two months I have been making a summary study of the history of philosophy from Thales of Miletus to the present day. . . . I have found nothing serious in the course of this great gallimaufry! . . . Talent, genius, remarkable personalities to whom we owe discoveries—yes: but not a single system of philosophy which bears scrutiny. . . . With morality it is different. Socrates, that is to say Plato, Montaigne (admirable because he has no system) . . . but spiritualism, idealism, eclecticism, materialism, scepticism . . . all of it frankly useless! Stoicism formed *men*, despite its errors. . . . To sum up, true philosophy consists in this—examine the known facts, extend scientific knowledge and ignore *entirely* everything that is not proven and exact. That is positivism, the only rational philosophy, and it is odd that the human spirit should have taken nearly 3,000 years to realise it.'

Poor Bizet! So intent on not being the simple, instinctive artist that he was by nature, and so impressed by the intellectual gifts which he lacked himself. There is a certain truculence in his rejection of idealistic philosophy, a truculence which is easily explained by a passage from his earlier letter to Galabert (October 1866), quoted on page 47. There he ends his philosophising by saying:

'Look here, I am a wretched philosopher, as you see. Well, I assure you that I should write better music if I believed in all these lies. . . . art declines as reason advances. . . . '

The intellectual arguments for materialism seemed unanswerable to him: but he felt that materialism meant the death of art, and art was the one thing he understood and loved. And so, in theory, he became a cynic, like many people who cannot reconcile the arguments prompted by their heads with the feelings in their hearts. But it was a strange cynic who could write only a month before:

'An extraordinary change is going on in me. I am changing my skin, as an artist and as a man; I am becoming purer, better, I can feel it! There, I shall find something in myself, if I look hard enough.'

He would have been wiser to leave philosophy alone: it merely puzzled and depressed him. But he had no commission for a new work and the only original composition he was working on did not satisfy his conscience nor exhaust his energies. He had returned to the piano of which he had shown promise of becoming so brilliant a virtuoso at the Conservatoire: and during 1868 he wrote a *Nocturne*, *Chasse Fantastique*, and the *Variations chromatiques de concert*. His piano style was plainly more distinguished in performance than in composition. His old teacher, Marmontel, wrote warmly of him as a performer.

'His execution was always firm and brilliant, and possessed an ample sonority, a variety of timbre and nuance which gave his playing an inimitable charm. He excelled in the modulation of tone and the art of making it supple by means of delicate or heavy finger-pressure. Like a truly accomplished performer, he could make a melody stand out in full relief, enveloping it at the same time in a veil of diaphonous harmony, whose undulating or vigorous rhythm he moulded to the melodic part. The charm of his touch, smooth and persuasive, was irresistible.' But the most flattering tribute of all was paid him by Liszt, whom he met at dinner with his old master Halévy one evening in 1861. After dinner, Liszt sat down at the piano and played one of his latest compositions, remarking when he had finished it that there were only two pianists alive who could master its great technical difficulties—Von Bülow and himself. Then, turning to Bizet, of whose technique he had heard, he said: 'Did you notice that passage?'—roughly sketching on the piano what he meant. Bizet sat down and played the passage perfectly, and Liszt was so impressed that he made him play the whole work from the copy which he had with him. The performance was astonishingly brilliant, and Liszt praised Bizet to the skies. ' My young friend ', he said, ' I thought that there were only two of us who could master the difficulties of this piece. There are three, and in justice I must add that the youngest is the boldest and the most brilliant.'

Berlioz, too, in his article on *Les Pêcheurs de Perles* (*Les Débats*, October 8, 1863) praised Bizet's powers of reading a score from sight.

' M. Bizet, prize-winner of the Institut, has been to Rome: he has returned without having forgotten music . . . he is an incomparable scorereader . . . almost unparalleled since the days of Liszt and Mendelssohn.'

It is disappointing to find less force and originality in his piano compositions than such testimonials would lead one to expect. The Nocturne is no more than salon music, modelled rather upon Liszt than Chopin, conventionally brilliant but of no musical interest. The *Chasse Fantastique*, dedicated to Marmontel, is again quite undistinguished. As its title suggests, it represents a *Walpurgisnacht* in the woods, the hunting calls interrupted by wild semi-quaver passages, chromatic scales and arpeggios of the diminished seventh. It is little more than a conventional *morceau de concert*, owing much to Stephen Heller in particular and, in general, to the French conception of German romanticism. The *Variations chromatiques* are on a rather higher plane. In July 1868 Bizet wrote to Galabert:

' I have just finished some *Grandes Variations*

Chromatiques for the piano, on the chromatic
theme I sketched out this last winter, I confess
that I am absolutely content with this composition. It is treated very boldly, as you will see.
Then a *Nocturne* to which I attach importance.'
The theme consists of a chromatic scale starting
on C, at first ascending and then descending, with
a C pedal throughout. The first three variations are
schematically closely similar: the chromatic scale is
in the left hand and above it is set a rather elegant
air in C minor, at first (Var. 1) simply and then
ornamented with quaver triplets (Var. 2) and rushing
scale passages (Var. 3). The fourth variation is in
the form of a brilliant *polonaise de concert* with the
chromatic scale still in the left hand. In the fifth the
theme is heard *tremolando* in the right hand, while the
left introduces a new, broader theme in C minor.
The chromatic scale is heard in the bass again in
the sixth, short emotional phrases in the right hand
standing out over thick, broken chords in demi-
semi-quavers in the left. Both hands are in unison
in the seventh, the theme occurring in the inner
parts while a *tremolando* C pedal forms the setting.
The eighth variation is in the major and consists
of a winning, Schumannesque air over the chromatic
bass of the theme. The ninth, also in the major, is
marked *legierissimo*, semi-quaver figures playing
lightly over a simple accompaniment which em-
bodies the chromatic theme. The tenth is a simple
C major *alla polacca*: but the eleventh is a more
florid, emotional movement, with pianistic ornamentation and *fioriture* in the manner of Chopin's
nocturnes. The twelfth, too, with its unison triplets,
is reminiscent of the last movement of Chopin's B

flat minor Sonata. The thirteenth is a variation, in the major, of the fifth variation: and the fourteenth is a simple lyrical movement in the style of the *Kinderscenen* of Schumann. The Coda is also strongly suggestive of Schumann, fragmentary reminiscences of several variations appearing in a fantasy (*melancolico, quasi recitativo*) or improvisation on the chromatic scale, until the theme dies away beneath a little sobbing phrase, only blazing out into the grand manner at the very end.

Ex. 20

The six *Chants du Rhin* for the pianoforte were written under the influence of Schumann and Mendelssohn, and they are a French blend of the *Kinderscenen* and *Lieder ohne Worte*. The child-like naïveté of Schumann and Mendelssohn does not easily wear French clothes, and the *Chants du Rhin* are rather artificial. The best is No. 4, *La Bohémienne*, in which Bizet ceased to imitate German *Innigkeit* and drew a simple musical character sketch, full of verve and gaiety. *Les Rêves* and *Les Confidences* are unhappy translations from the German. *Le Départ* and *Le Retour* are more naturally in Bizet's manner, gay and exterior with points of wit and sentiment never too heavily underlined. Apart from these Bizet wrote only two *morceaux de salon* for piano solo, *Venise* and *Marine*, both in a style suited to the 'lady-amateurs' of the day, and now mercifully extinct. The *Jeux d'Enfants* for piano duet will be dealt with later, in their chronological place.

On June 3, 1869, Bizet married Geneviève Halévy. To please his wife and in gratitude to her father's memory, he now set to work to finish Halévy's unfinished opera, *Noë*, which entailed not only the harmonisation and orchestration of much that was already existent in sketch form, but also the writing of a complete last act. As always, Bizet had plans for several new works. *Calendal*, a libretto by Paul Fevrier, seems hardly to have been begun, since du Locle did not care for it. A libretto by Philippe Gilles, based on Richardson's *Clarissa Harlowe*, was 'hardly started' in February 1870 when he wrote that his work on Sardou's *Griselidis* was 'very well ahead'. In 1870 he was a member of the Prix de Rome jury, a mark of official recognition: then came the war. In 1859, when he was at Rome and French troops were fighting the Austrians in the north of Italy, Bizet had been an ardent patriot, the full force of his nationalist fervour being directed against England. On May 9 he wrote to his family:

' All I can do is to wish our armies every success. Every good Frenchman will do as much. Austria will quickly be beaten; what will be more difficult is *England*! In any case, let us hope.'

And in August his Anglophobia reached white-heat:
'People begin to fear a war with England. I
would give two years of my life to conquer this
modern Carthage.'
But in 1870 Bizet had seen too much of life to
believe that war could be anything but disastrous.
'And our poor philosophy, our dreams of
universal peace, international brotherhood,
human co-operation! No, in place of that tears,
blood, piles of carnage, endless and numberless
crimes! I cannot tell you, my friend, into what
misery I am plunged by all these horrors. I am
a Frenchman, I know: but I cannot altogether
forget that I am a human being. This war will
cost humanity 500,000 lives. As for France, she
will lose everything in it (*elle y laissera tout*).'
This was written to Edmond Galabert in August
1870, war having been declared in July. The armis-
tice was signed on January 28, 1871, and was
followed on March 18 by the setting up of the Paris
Commune, which was not defeated until May 29,
with the accompanying massacre of 20,000 Parisians.
Bizet had finished work on Halévy's *Noë* in November 1869, and had since then been working, though
without committing anything but rough sketches
to paper, on *Griselidis* and *Clarissa Harlowe*. During
the war and the Commune he can have done very
little work; but fortunately a series of letters written
to his mother-in-law, Mme. Halévy, give us a
picture of his reactions to political events. He was
living outside Paris, at Le Vésinet, but near enough
to know the trend of events in the city. In April
(during the Commune) he wrote:
'Ten years ago I believed in men, I went

about amongst them and, frankly, enjoyed it. Now I am not a misanthrope, I am indifferent: I do not hate, I merely despise. I am not badly off as I stand at present. The road I have taken is long, but I know where it takes me. Some who seem near the goal will never reach it, whereas I shall, if life becomes normal again. Besides, I am one of the twenty or thirty people in the world whom I respect! That in itself is something.'

On the 19th of the same month he wrote:

'Once the insurrection is defeated—and it cannot be long now, despite the stupidity of certain generals—everything will be in a state of flux. The clericals will exact bitter vengeance and the cruelty of these gentlemen is well known. Between the excesses of the " reds " and the "whites" there will be no place for decent people. Music will have no future here. I shall have to go abroad—Italy, England, or America? '

He retained an unusually clear head about Germany —admitting that the occupying Prussians behaved well, and not hesitating to praise to Mme. Halévy the genius of Wagner, although he realised that ' the whole of nineteenth century German thought is incarnate in this man ':

'It is the fate of these great geniuses to be mis-understood by their contemporaries. Wagner is no friend of mine and I hold him in but mediocre esteem: but I cannot forget the immense pleasure I owe to his revolutionary genius. The charm of his music is inexpressible. It is all voluptuous-ness, tenderness, love! If I could play you this music for a week, you would be madly in love with it! . . . The Germans, who, alas, are at least our equals in music, understand that Wagner is one of their strongest pillars. The whole of nineteenth century German -thought is incarnate in this man.'

Perhaps the most charming index of his unhappiness during these months of war and revolution is a dream which he relates in a letter to his friend Guiraud:

'Last night I dreamed that we were all at Naples, in a delightful villa, living under a purely artistic government. The Senate consisted of Beethoven, Michelangelo, Shakespeare, Giorgione and so on. The Garde Nationale was replaced by a vast orchestra under the command of Litolff. The vote was withheld from fools, knaves, intriguers and ignoramuses. That is to say, it was the least universal suffrage imaginable. Geneviève was rather too well disposed towards Goethe: but in spite of this, waking was very bitter.'

No dream of 'escape' could be more charming, nor throw a pleasanter light on the deepest desires and ideals of the dreamer. Whether it was the influence of his wife or the effect of the war and revolution, Bizet emerged in 1872 as a fully mature artist in a sense that he had never been before. In the summer of 1871 he received a commission from the Opéra Comique to set a one-act libretto by Louis Gallet, *Djamileh*, and, since this was performed on May 22 of 1872, Bizet must have spent most of the autumn and winter at work upon it. The days of working for publishers were over: he was settled with a wife whom he adored and an infant son, in a quiet villa where he could devote himself without interruption to his composition. The circumstances were at last ideal and the quality of his new work makes it clear how much Bizet profited from them.

CHAPTER V

THE poem of *Djamileh* is based on the *Namouna* of
Alfred de Musset, which gave Edouard Lalo an
idea for a ballet ten years later. Bizet had no luck
with his libretti. *Djamileh* is an attempt to dramatise
a quite undramatic poem and dramatically it is a
failure. *Namouna* is an oriental monologue in the
style of Byron, and its charm and point lie in the
cynical and witty observations of the poet, even
though those observations had already been made
by Byron in *Don Juan*. The story is simple. Haroun,
caliph of Cairo, is an unhappy and disillusioned
voluptuary, who makes a point of changing his
mistress regularly every month: the new mistress is
supplied by his servant, Splendiano, who often takes
over his master's cast-off women at the end of their
month of service. Djamileh, unlike most of Haroun's
mistresses, falls deeply in love with her master, and
this causes the complications which form the subject
of the play. The overture is longer and more
developed than any Bizet had hitherto written. It
opens with an *allegro* (*Mouvement de marche*) in C
minor, with an episode, oddly reminiscent of
Chopin's étude in A flat major, leading back to a
restatement of the open march. This forms the first
half of the overture. The second half consists of an
E flat major theme set above a simple accompaniment figure, leading eventually back to the opening
march and a coda. The form is not satisfactory: it is
a rondo with one of the episodes (the E flat theme

at the opening of the second half) so extended as to
become almost as important as the main theme.
Harmonically, it is more daring than anything Bizet
had written hitherto (it was widely held to be
'Wagnerian', needless to say), though its harmony
is not based on any revolutionary theory but only
on an extensive use of the *appoggiatura*, or passing
note, as in such phrases.

Ex. 21

The curtain goes up on Haroun and Splendiano,
the master lying on a sofa smoking while his servant
sits at a low table writing. In the wings are a small
chorus and orchestra, the tenors and basses humming *à bouches fermées*, while the women sing:

Le soleil s'en va; ramène ta voile,
  C'est la fin du jour,
Et vers l'Orient la première étoile
  S'allume, invitant notre âme à l'àmour.

The orchestra has only pianissimo supporting
chords, but a *tambour de basque* keeps up a persistent
rhythm ♪♪♪ ♪♪♪♪ which gives the oriental atmosphere. The song is repeated, and as it dies away the
second time Haroun watches the smoke curling up
from his hookah and sees in the white shapes which
it forms the vague figures of women, fading as the

smoke mingles with the last rays of the sun. He ceases his rêverie and the orchestra takes over the expression of emotion in a *mélodrame*, as the slave Djamileh crosses the stage, casts a lingering look of love on her master, who does not even notice her, and disappears, as the chorus takes up the evening song again. This is followed by a discussion between Splendiano and his master, whom he warns, sententiously, of the power of love. Haroun declares that his heart is a desert which will need more than Splendiano imagines to make it blossom in love. Bizet catches perfectly the good-humoured pretentiousness of the old servant and the blasé man-of-the-world air (*legèrement, railleur*) of Haroun. Splendiano tentatively praises Djamileh's beauty: but Haroun is not interested and declares that in any case she has a rival. ' A rival? Who? ' asks Splendiano, agog with inquisitiveness. ' *L'inconnue!*', answers Haroun, and breaks into a charming panegyric of promiscuity, the piquancy and excitement of making love to a woman of whom one knows nothing, and for whom one feels nothing but titillated desire. He is quite ready to hand over Djamileh to Splendiano, and only asks him to choose her successor for him, sadly explaining that he has no particular preference of nationality or complexion, that he is in love with love, not with any particular woman or class of women. Splendiano, who is himself in love with Djamileh, is overjoyed: and the scene ends with a repetition of Haroun's song. Djamileh enters, pale and unhappy-looking, and Haroun dismisses Splendiano. He asks Djamileh why she is sad, and she tells him her dream, of being terrified by a storm at sea, of turning to him for

protection and finding him not there: she has a
presentiment . . . Haroun is disturbed, for he never
lets his mistresses know the terms on which they
come to him, and he foresees emotional complications in getting rid of Djamileh. Now, however,
she is ready to be consoled, and as Splendiano
returns with the servants bringing supper, she
brightens, ready to forget her dream and believe in
Haroun's love. He offers her her liberty, but at once
she becomes sad again and she tells him gently
that she could conceive no greater happiness than
being in his house; Splendiano interrupts her with
praise of the wine, and Haroun begs her, if she will
not drink, at least to sing to them. Splendiano hands
her a lute and after a few introductory bars she
begins the *ghazel* of Nour-Eddin, King of Lahore.
It is a simple song of unrequited love, and Djamileh
sings for Haroun, her Nour-Eddin, of whose love
she is no longer certain. There are two verses, with
the rhythm 〈22a〉 persisting in the
accompaniment, and after each comes the refrain:

Ex.22

82

la —— la la la

After the second refrain Haroun, embarrassed,
interrupts Djamileh and asks her for a gayer song.
She adapts herself to his mood, and with the two
men she joins in a trio praising wine and song—
brilliant, mundane and elegant. Once again the
orchestra plays a *mélodrame* after the trio, while
Haroun gives Djamileh a necklace, bidding her be
happy and not forget him, making at the same time
a sign to Splendiano to show that it is the ' end of
the comedy ', and he does not wish to see her again.
Djamileh is puzzled by his words, but Haroun is
called away by his friends who have come to spend
the evening gambling with him. Bizet characterises
them and their leering interest in Djamileh, who
remains unveiled in their presence, in a fussy and
noisy chorus. To their questions Haroun answers
nonchalantly that the beauty is Djamileh, and as he
speaks a single oboe plays the theme of the *ghazel*,
as if in reproach: but he is set on his pleasure and
calls his friends to the tables, as the muezzin, he
says, is calling the faithful to prayer. They disappear
—with them Splendiano—and soon their voices
are heard in the wings, singing an unaccompanied
chorus comparing the fortune of the tables to the
caprice of women—a brilliantly effective device,

leaving Djamileh alone on the stage. Splendiano returns and she asks him to do her a favour—allow her to disguise herself as Haroun's new mistress and try and win his love by her devotion; if she fails, she will give herself to Splendiano. He agrees. This is spoken dialogue: but now, when Splendiano leaves her, Djamileh sings a broken-hearted *lamento*, half-foreseeing the failure of her ruse and despairing of the future. The introductory chords must have caused searching of hearts among the fault-finding critics

Ex.23

who would at once raise the cry of Wagnerism.

The slave dealer is then announced to Haroun, and he enters with his wares, to the *mouvement de marche* of the overture. Haroun is not interested in the women for sale, and horrifies the merchant by leaving the choice of his new mistress to Splendiano. The most beautiful of the girls is chosen to dance before the buyer. She begins, at first slowly, and the chorus formed of Haroun's friends, the other slaves and musicians, whisper:

Froide et lente,
Indolente,
Et les yeux assoupis,
Elle pose
Son pied rose

84

Sur les fleurs du tapis.
Et comme elle,
Solennelle,
La musique s'endort
in open fifths beneath ambiguous phrases of the
dance, perpetually hovering, as it seems to Western
ears, between major and minor.

Ex.24
Andantino

Then the dance becomes more lively and reaches
an almost orgiastic wildness, the women's voices
punctuating the dancers' movements with cries of
'lou', finally sinking down again to the calm of the
opening. In spoken dialogue Haroun gives Splendiano an indifferent command to buy the girl, and
he and his friends return to their tables, accompanied
in the orchestra by the original passage which
introduced the gamers. Splendiano is beside himself
with joy, thinking that he is sure of Djamileh, and
bursts into a comic song of senile lechery, as he
pictures, breathless with excitement, his conquest
of Djamileh—a fine piece of characterisation in the
tradition of Mozart's Osmin. Haroun returns from
the tables to find the girl whom he takes to be his
new mistress waiting for him. It is Djamileh,
heavily veiled and trembling with suspense, and the
brusque change (as he thinks) from the provocative-
ness of her dance to her present timidity puzzles
Haroun. He speaks his thoughts to Splendiano, as
the theme of the dance is heard from a single oboe.

He tries to take the girl in his arms, but she slips
away.

Haroun is intrigued, hands his purse to Splendiano,
telling him to take his place at the tables and refusing
to listen to a word from him. Splendiano leaves
them alone, muttering anxiously and trying to
persuade himself that Haroun will dismiss Djamileh,
after all, as soon as he discovers her ruse. During
this dialogue the orchestra starts to set the stage,
as it were, for the scene between the two lovers—
Djamileh fighting desperately for her love, and
Haroun engaged, as he thinks, on one of his many
piquant adventures. In the duet which follows he is
concerned entirely with his own sensations; he has
all the vanity and egoism of the professional Don
Juan, and he cannot imagine that any woman will
make difficulties with him except by way of coquetry.
Djamileh begs the darkness to come to her help,
and refuses to unveil. Haroun loses patience when
he sees that she is in earnest. 'The slave you are
replacing was less difficult, and I loved her . . . ',
he says. In a flash Djamileh answers bitterly, ' If
you loved her, why did you send her away? ' but
before she has finished speaking, regrets her words
and fears they may have betrayed her. Haroun's
cynical declaration of his voluptuary's faith, harking
back to the supper music of the third scene, makes
Djamileh weep, and Haroun is sincerely touched
for a moment. She moves away from him, as he
tries to kiss her, and as she moves her veil slips and
a ray of light catches her face. Haroun recognises
her and is profoundly moved in spite of himself,
trying at once to reason himself out of his emotion.
Djamileh despairs of winning him, and in a last

effort of desperation she sings the third verse of the *ghazel* of Nour-Eddin, which Haroun had interrupted earlier in the evening: but before she reaches the refrain her emotion is too much for her, and she turns to Haroun in direct supplication. He struggles against his own feelings and finally steels himself to reject her. Broken-hearted, she bids him farewell and moves away, while in the orchestra is heard the phrase to which she first appeared. Before she reaches the door she stumbles, and is only prevented from falling by Haroun taking her in his arms. His resistance is conquered and the curtain falls on a rather banal love duet, the weakest point of the whole work, the discomforted Splendiano and Haroun's friends appearing in the doorway as Haroun and Djamileh pass out of the room in each other's arms.

Djamileh is not great music, but of its simple kind it is a masterpiece. Here for the first time Bizet's touch was absolutely sure: he was no longer finding himself, and no longer the battle-gound of opposing influences, one moment Gounod, the next Verdi or Meyerbeer. *Djamileh* is his first completely original work, his own in its failings as well as in its felicities. The subject was not happy, carrying a slight odour of moral ambiguity without any compensating advantage of dramatic value. Haroun is hardly a dramatic figure, for he has no strong feelings of any kind: and Djamileh has surely only postponed her fate when she wins him again at the end of the opera. She herself is a charming figure: and in her music Bizet shows for the first time his ability to write genuine and original love music, without having recourse to Gounod or any other model.

The exotic element is treated with perfect taste, suggested rather than underlined except in the slave-girl's dance. The orchestral interludes, or *mélodrames*, are really expressive and dramatic, without assuming too large an importance or disturbing the balance of the whole work. In spite of this, *Djamileh* was a complete failure, only running for four performances. *Les Pêcheurs de Perles* had been given eighteen performances, *La Jolie Fille de Perth* twenty-one; hitherto, in fact, the success of Bizet's works had been in inverse proportion to their merit. Nevertheless Ernest Reyer was, as so often, penetrating enough in his criticism to see the real merit of *Djamileh*. ' The musician who falters as he makes a step forward is more interesting than the musician who shows us the ease with which he steps backwards.'

Djamileh was performed in May and rather less than six months later Bizet's name was again before the public. Alphonse Daudet's Provençal play *L'Arlésienne* was given its first performance on October 1 at the Odéon, with incidental music provided by Bizet. The theatre orchestra of the Odéon was small (twenty-six players[1]), and not too efficient: and this circumstance to a certain extent dictated the scale and technical difficulty of Bizet's music. Fortunately, he was delivered from the additional complication of singers. Bizet himself supported the choruses with a small harmonium in the wings or he was sometimes relieved by his publisher's son, Antony Choudens.

[1] Bizet disposed his orchestra thus: 2 flutes, 1 oboe (cor anglais), 1 clarinet, 2 bassoons; 1 saxophone, 2 horns, 1 drum; 7 violins, 1 viola, 5 violoncelli, 2 double-basses.

The Prelude opens with an old Provençal march, traditionally known as the Marche des Rois (*Marcho dei Rei*), but also as the Marche de Turenne. It is announced *ff* by the strings and wood-wind, alone in unison, and this simple statement is followed by three variations of the 'melodic' kind, in which the theme remains unaltered, and only its harmonisation and setting are varied. The original theme is stated in C minor, and after the third variation in C major, the full orchestra plays the theme in its original minor form, but in full orchestral dress, and as magnificently adorned as the nature of the theme and the smallness of the orchestra will allow. There then follows an Andante section in A flat major, a more lyrical and tender passage which is connected during the play with the character of l'Innocent, the mentally only half-awakened child whose dullness and retarded development are regarded almost religiously by his family. The prelude closes with the sinister and passionate theme of Frédéri, the boy whose infatuation for the 'woman of Arles' and its tragic dénouement are the theme of the play. This theme is closely related to that of the *mélodrame* in *Djamileh* (Scene 1), where the orchestra depicts the slave-girl's hopeless passion for her master: and, in this second form, it seems to be as near as Bizet ever went to justifying the critics' repeated charges of 'Wagnerism.'

Ex. 25

The curtain goes up on the courtyard of a Provençal farm in the Camargue kept by the widowed Rose
Mamai and her father-in-law, Francet Mamai. Rose
Mamai has two sons, Frédéri (the elder) and
l'Innocent (the younger son), not fully mentally
developed and largely cared for by the old shepherd
Balthazar. The first three *mélodrames* underline the
lyrical importance which Daudet attached to the
character of l'Innocent, neglected by his mother but
full of a simple, saint-like awareness which gives
him an insight into the silent development of the
tragedy and finally blossoms, as old Balthazar had
prophesied, into a spiritual and mental maturity
of which the normal characters of the play are
incapable. The theme of l'Innocent is beautifully
suggestive, in its incomplete form of the stunted
sweetness of the child's character, and in its complete form of the full power inherent in that sweetness. His mother, Rose Mamai, can think only of
her elder son and his forthcoming engagement to
the ' woman of Arles ', whom the rest of the family
have not seen: she is still anxious until her brother,
captain of a small boat on the Rhône, arrives from
Arles with the news that he has seen and approved
the girl and her parents. Meanwhile Vivette, a girl
of the neighbouring village, is hopelessly in love
with Frédéri, though her secret is guessed by none
of the family except l'Innocent and old Balthazar.
She has come to help with the silk-worm harvest on
the farm, and finds herself in the middle of the
festivities celebrating Frédéri's engagement. As old
Balthazar sits in the courtyard and the family sing
and drink in the house, there arrives a stranger
asking to speak to old Francet. He will not enter,

but when Francet comes out to him he explains, half defiant and half shamefaced, that Frédéri's fiancée has been his mistress for two years and that he is unwilling to give her up, though the family and the girl herself are anxious for the marriage. He unwillingly hands over two of her letters, which prove that he tells the truth, and goes. Francet turns to go back to the farm, when Frédéri comes out, flushed with excitement and pleasure, bidding him drink to his Arlésienne. Francet blurts out the truth and Frédéri falls as if he were stunned, while from the farm the chorus bursts out ironically again, until the curtain falls to the wild phrase of Frédéri's tragic love played by the orchestra. Bizet manages the contrasts beautifully in this last scene, the gay, banal chorus of the farm-workers set first against the sombre music which announces the arrival of Mitifio, the stranger

Ex.26

with its mixture of hesitancy and urgent fatefulness; and then against the orchestra's cry of despairing love, as Frédéri's dreams are shattered.

The scene of the second act is the Vaccarès marsh, near the farm, where the captain is stalking snipe. Before the curtain rises the orchestra gives the atmosphere of the countryside at midday, heavy with heat, but still mysterious and empty. In the distance rises a chorus of the silk-gatherers, wordless and alive with almost animal rhythm, shifting adroitly from key to key but making use of a single melodic phrase, which goes back to Leonard's *bolero d'amour* in *Vasco da Gama*, but looks forward, too, to *Carmen*. Rose Mamai and Vivette are discussing Frédéri, who has disappeared for the morning without explanation. They are both anxious that he may try to do away with himself in the mood of unshakeable gloom which has settled on him since the breaking of his engagement with the woman of Arles. His mother hopes to cure him by finding another woman, and Vivette, whom she approves, is only too willing to try her hand, but feels herself incapable of the brilliance and coquetry which fascinated Frédéri in her rival. As Balthazar enters with l'Innocent and Vivette goes to look for Frédéri, the orchestra plays a few bars of *mélodrame*, not the theme connected hitherto with l'Innocent, but a more passionate, human theme, tender and strong, which gathers together the strands of Rose Mamai's adoration for her son and Vivette's selfless devotion. Rose and Balthazar discuss the situation, and Balthazar rebukes her so frankly for neglecting l'Innocent that, as she goes, she tells him that he should have been a priest, his sermons would have been excellent: and then, turning back in a sudden rush of love, she seizes l'Innocent and strains him to her, while the orchestra plays a variation of the earlier theme, faster and more passionate, but sinking quickly to a melancholy, half-sinister close. Left alone with Balthazar, l'Innocent goes to look for something to eat, and, pushing open the door of a shed, finds Frédéri, dishevelled and miserable. He has been hiding from ' all these women ', has heard his mother's conversation with Vivette, but remained hidden, wanting only to be left alone. In the orchestra returns the theme of his tragic passion, but in a meditative, self-torturing form, which almost seems to look forward to the harmonies of César Franck.

Ex.27

Frédéri has got hold of Mitifio's letters, and tortures himself reading the passionate protestations of the woman of Arles to her lover. In the distance the cry of the shepherds announces the sunset, and Balthazar goes to fold his sheep. L'Innocent tries to distract his brother by telling him one of Balthazar's stories, but gets confused at the very start, and as Frédéri turns the knife in his own heart, reading the ' je me suis donnée a toi toute entière ' which the woman he loves has written to another man, l'Innocent begins to doze. The *Er dou Guet*, played by the orchestra as a *berceuse*, is a Provençal air chosen by Bizet not only for its local associations, but also for its gentle sleepiness, its nodding repetitions suiting exactly the drowsy efforts of l'Innocent to remember Balthazar's story. As Frédéri sits lost in ' his ' love letters and bitter memories of the past, Vivette comes up behind him and, in a pathetic attempt to follow Rose's advice, playfully throws a handful of flowers in Frédéri's face. For the moment he has the illusion that it is his old love: and his bitter disappointment makes him doubly hard on Vivette, when she tells him openly that she loves him and that his mother wants her to win him from his depression. He answers brutally that he does not, and never will, love her; and as Rose enters, he runs quickly away. There is the sound of a shot, and both Rose and Vivette think for a moment that he has killed himself: but it is only the Captain, who has missed his snipe for the twentieth time, and the scene ends with the chorus, which was heard at the beginning, sounding again in the distance.

The second scene is preceded by an entr'acte (later adapted as an *O Salutaris*, which has done Bizet much discredit), the main melody of which is a broad, simple and slightly sentimental melody given to the saxophone and horn, and accompanied by the strings. The curtain goes up on the kitchen of the farm. Frédéri's mother has called a family council and puts before them the suggestion that, rather than see Frédéri pine away for love of his Arles woman, they should consent to let him marry her. Old Francet is horrified, and Balthazar declares he would sooner see his grandson dead than bringing such dishonour on his family. Rose is just turning to him in fury when Frédéri appears and declares that he will not bring disgrace on them all, but will

94

try and forget his old love and marry Vivette: and the act closes with Rose embracing her future daughter-in-law, as the theme of the entr'acte is heard (*tremolando*) in the strings of the orchestra, recalling the rêverie theme in *Pêcheurs de Perles* which it resembles in melody as well as orchestration. The following Intermezzo is one of the most popular of Bizet's compositions, the brilliant C minor opening contrasting well with the air of the clarinet and saxophone and the light-hearted gaiety of the whole movement preparing the audience for the betrothal of Frédéri and Vivette. Before the curtain goes up on Act III a *carillon* sounds in the orchestra, a persistent, deafening, thoroughly rural music which ceases as the curtain rises on the Castelet courtyard, filled with workmen and servants who are busy preparing the celebrations, for it is the feast of St. Éloi, patron of the silk-worm gatherers, as well as Frédéri's engagement to Vivette. Balthazar enters, hot and tired, and is sitting in the courtyard when Vivette arrives with her grandmother, Mère Renaud. She and Balthazar had known each other when they were young, loved each other and parted, for she was already married. They have never seen each other since, but neither has forgotten.

Two flutes, accompanied by the viola, announce Mère Renaud's entrance with a tender, reflective melody, peaceful but poignant. At first she does not see Balthazar, who is sitting overcome with emotion in a corner of the courtyard. Then she catches sight of him, and is overcome in her turn. They tell each other their uneventful life stories, how neither has ever forgotten or ceased to love. Their gentle love-making is accompanied by the strings in a *mélodrame* of a perfect beauty and pathos, which shows beyond a doubt the instinctive fineness, the miniaturist's gift for the *mot juste* which Bizet had developed. There is no trace of sentimentality, for these two had denied themselves for a lifetime: their emotion, and Bizet's expression of it, is crystal clear and fresh as dew. She asks him if he will kiss her, *toute vieille et crevassée par le temps que je suis là*: and then the whole company goes into the farm, as the flutes repeat their original theme. The stage is left empty. From within comes the strains of the Intermezzo: and, that finished, Frédéri and Vivette come out alone. He assures her of his love: she questions him about the Arles woman and he swears he has forgotten her. As they embrace and wander off the stage harp and clarinet play the theme of their love until they disappear into the evening. It is the moment of lyrical calm before the storm of the tragedy gathers. Mitifio appears, asking for his letters. Balthazar comes out and questions him. Mitifio is to elope with his mistress in a few days, he is intoxicated by his passion for her, though he realises her worthlessness. Frédéri and Vivette have wandered back and hear Mitifio's last words. Frédéri sees red and seizes a hammer to rush on his rival. He is just prevented by Balthazar and his mother, who comes out of the farm at that moment, followed by a crowd of peasants who strike up the Farandole, dancing and singing gaily to St. Eloi. This is the end of Scene I.

Before the curtain goes up on Scene 2 the orchestra plays as entr'acte the themes of the two brothers, first Frédéri—sombre, passionate, youthfully tragic; and then l'Innocent, this time fully developed in its tenderness and intense simplicity. Then the curtain goes up on the *Magnanerie*, where the silk-worms are kept, a great barn-like building connected with the farm itself. Off the stage the celebrations are still going on, the Farandole mingling with the chorus of the Three Kings (*Prélude*). Rose Mamai is alone at first, troubled and anxious: she is soon joined by Frédéri, who complains of the heat and noise in the house. She begs him to confide in her: but he persists in saying that his attack on Mitifio was only a last flare-up of his old passion, which is now dead for ever. He goes into the bedroom which he shares with his brother, and Rose is left alone, more rather than less anxious for her talk with him. L'Innocent creeps out of the room to her and astonishes her by the grasp he shows of his brother's misery. He is perfectly ' awakened ' now, and able to comfort and reassure his mother, telling her to call him no longer 'l'Innocent' but Janet, his proper name. He goes back to the bedroom, and Rose, after listening a moment at the door, tries to reassure herself. ' *Non, non, ce n'est pas possible! Dieu ne m'a pas rendu un enfant pour m'en enlever un autre!* ' she says to herself, and goes to the curtained corner where she has been sleeping to be near to Frédéri. In the orchestra is a gentle, almost religious passage, which leads after a pause, however, to the pianissimo statement of Frédéri's theme.

The door of the bedroom opens and Frédéri appears: he has struggled with himself all night and can bear it no longer, he is determined to end it all. He climbs by a staircase leading to the roof overlooking the courtyard, and as he climbs his mother rushes to catch hold of him. But she is too late and, as she looks down with horror on to his mangled body in the courtyard, Frédéri's theme sounds for the last time—loud, wild, passionate, and infinitely tragic—and the curtain falls.

With *L'Arlésienne* Bizet took that step forward which converted him from a gifted, immature second-ranker among the composers of his day to a mature and independent artist, a late-flowering talent which promised to blossom into something like genius. Daudet's play was criticised on the score of not being dramatic enough; but its erring on the side of lyricism, its concentration on the power of 'evocation' rather than direct presentation of each scene and situation fitted it the more perfectly for Bizet's music. From the very beginning, when he evoked Italy in *Don Procopio* and Ceylon in *Pêcheurs de Perles*, Bizet had shown his peculiar talent for exotic atmospheres, the suggestion (never underlined) of a world of feeling and physical being which was foreign, alien, different. In Provence the Northern Frenchman has a foreign country at his gates, even within his walls: and eight years before the appearance of *L'Arlésienne* Gounod, in collaboration with the Provençal poet Frédéric Mistral, had already carried Provence with his unfailing charm and skill to the operatic stage. *Mireille* is one of Gounod's most successful operas, alive and gay, as innocent of pretentiousness and banality as a child; but its dramatic quality is far below that of *L'Arlésienne*. Its rather similar love story is vitiated by the unconvincing interpolation of a supernatural element (Tavenne) and Ourrias, who plays Mitifio's rôle, is a blustering stage villain with none of Mitifio's humanity. Gounod, too, uses

Provence as so much local colour: for all its grace his music evokes a temperate, smiling landscape, not the burnt, desolate grandeur of the Camargue; and his Mireille is as much a Norman as she is a Provençal.

Daudet's characters are Provençal to the bone, they are part of the landscape, simple but mysterious, rugged and tender, fatally and unshowily tragic. Bizet caught Daudet's spirit in every detail of his music. His tenderness never becomes sentimental except in the music which accompanies Frédéri's forced and unreal love for Vivette. All his passion was given to the woman of Arles: he could spare nothing but superficial tenderness for Vivette, and the effort he made to forget the one and to form an idealistic love for the other broke him. Bizet's music for the Frédéri-Vivette relationship is touching, conventional, absolutely pure and fundamentally trivial. But the devotion of Mère Renaud and Balthazar, which had survived a lifetime of separation undiminished, evoked from him a very different music, bone-sincere and owing nothing to conventional formulae, as firm and as un-saccharine as the other is weak and maudlin. And behind the play of characters, underlying and conditioning each personality, is the countryside, burnt naked to the rock, intense, tragic. The chorus at the beginning of Act II, with its inexorable rhythm, the impersonality of its wordlessness and the beautiful bird-like solo melody, gathers together all the elements which Daudet felt in the Camargue countryside—lyricism side by side with tragedy, something sinister penetrating even the harmless work of the land. In contrast to this impersonality, which is partly symbolised among the characters by the old shepherd Balthazar, there stand the two brothers, violent contrasts in themselves and violently subjective in the terrifying objectivity of their setting. Bizet seems to have grasped, not by the intellect, but by the surer instinct of the artist, all these contrasts and nuances: for the first time in his life he had a worthy framework on which to work, and he showed himself perfectly appreciative.

After *L'Arlésienne* his name was unquestionably made, and he was certain not to lack for commissions.

On March 2 of the following year (1873) an orchestral suite, *Jeux d'enfants*, was given its first performance by Colonne. Its five numbers were chosen for orchestration by Bizet from a suite for piano duet which he had recently finished. The original suite contains twelve numbers: The Swing (Rêverie), The Top (Impromptu), The Doll (Berceuse), The Hobby Horse (Scherzo), The Shuttledore (Fantasy), Trumpet and Drum (March), Soap Bubbles (Rondino), Hide and Seek (Esquisse), Blindman's Buff (Nocturne), Leapfrog (Caprice), Little Husband, Little Wife (Duo), The Ball (Galop). The orchestral suite consists of Trumpet and Drum, The Doll, The Top, Little Husband, Little Wife, and The Ball. In the piano version Bizet wrote by far the best music he ever composed for the instrument. Here, as in *L'Arlésienne*, it was his gift as a miniaturist that was in demand, and the orchestration of the suite shows the same precision and fineness of touch which his work for the tiny Odéon orchestra had developed. As in *L'Arlésienne*, too, he entered apparently without any difficulty into the other, alien world—in this case, that of the child —in all its moods. Schumann's *Kinderscenen* are full of the ' grown-up's ' nostalgia of childhood, their premiss is sentimental and their popularity due to the universality of this sentimental nostalgia. Bizet's *Jeux d'enfants* are purely objective, genuinely childish in their alternate solemnity and triviality, never pathetic nor consciously innocent, never talking, as it were, ' baby language.' Schumann saw children with the eyes of a grown-up, and the *Kinderscenen* gain thereby in musical interest. Bizet, without Schumann's complication of character, could feel not only with, but like children: and *Jeux d'enfants* are therefore in the best sense childish.

Patrie, a concert overture which followed in 1874, is the exact antithesis of *Jeux d'Enfants*. Written nominally as a tone poem inspired by the Polish resistance against Russia, and bearing the title ' Bataille de Raclawice gagnée sur les Russes par Kosciuszko, 1792 ', the real inspiration was undoubtedly the French resistance to the Prussian invasion three years before. It is dedicated to Massenet, who was just making his debut as a composer (*Les Erinnyes* and *Marie Magdeleine* appeared in 1873). *Patrie* is not worthy of Bizet at the state of development he had now reached. It has no longer the moments of insincerity which disfigure *Pêcheurs de Perles* and so much of *La Jolie Fille de Perth*: the ideas are original but weak, and the whole work falls far below the heroic level set by its title. Bizet was not gifted for epic writing, and his attempted grandeur falls flat. *Patrie* has never had any great success, and is quite justifiably forgotten to-day. But Bizet could afford a minor failure in February 1874: for he had already received from the Opéra Comique the libretto of a new opera, a tale of Prosper Merimée arranged by Meilhac and Halévy, and he was hard at work, convinced that he had at last found the right subject for the perfect development of his composer's faculty. This time not only France, but the whole world, echoed his belief: the libretto was *Carmen*.

CHAPTER VI

THE libretto which Meilhac and Halévy constructed from Prosper Merimée's *conte* was not by any standards perfect, and probably seems more unforgivable now than in 1875. It was greatly abused at the time, it is true: but on grounds of moral depravity, while we find fault with its moral inoffensiveness as an act of treachery to Merimée. Meilhac and Halévy were, of course, bound to choose, and more or less bound to adapt, various episodes from Merimée's story, in order to construct not only a stage version of the story, but a stage version which could also be set to music and played at the Opéra Comique. The range of possibilities was therefore not large, and, all things considered, we may be grateful that the libretto of *Carmen* is as good as it is. It was impossible to put Merimée's Carmen on the nineteenth-century stage: she was by all accepted standards a *fille de Satan*, an unrepentant thief, liar and tart, unwashed and dressed in dirty and tawdry rags. As it was, the comparatively drawing-room figure drawn by Meilhac and Halévy was considered extremely improper, and *Carmen* was regarded as a most sophisticated and advanced entertainment to which not all men would take their wives and no man would take his daughters. Merimée's Don José was a brigand, utterly depraved by his passion for Carmen, though he began as a gawky, innocent young provincial from Navarre, with no idea of women but the 'blue-skirted, pigtailed village girls' of his province. Out of this single phrase of Merimée's, the librettists constructed the figure of Micaela, the conventional counterbalance to Carmen, the personification of innocence and as characterless as any personification must be. If they had only given her one fault, if she had only accepted the soldiers' invitation to wait for Don José in the guard-room! But the nineteenth century would be content with nothing less than perfection, and Meilhac and Halévy salved their consciences, overburdened with the guilt of portraying such a *fille damnée* as Carmen, by making of Micaela the perfect goody-goody, *une petite perfection* as Bizet had laughingly called himself. In Merimée's story Carmen has a husband, Garcia le Borgne, the biggest and most unqualified villain of the lot: the librettists shuddered and omitted even a reference to such a monster. Escamillo is modelled on the bullfighter Lucas, who in Merimée's story precipitated the *dénouement*, it is true, but not by stealing Carmen from Don José. Merimée's Carmen had not been faithful to José for more than a matter of weeks, and Lucas was only one of many promiscuities, some for love, many for money. Whether Bizet could have set Merimée's Carmen to music is doubtful: it is certain that no stage would have presented it until probably well into the twentieth century. As it was, Bizet had no very high standard for libretti and, seeing many opportunities in the poem offered him, was delighted with what he had. He was a *bon bourgeois*, with no literary education or natural literary taste, and he could understand Micaela and the Don José of Meilhac and Halévy:

their Carmen, though possibly not within his experience, needed only a little imagination, for Bizet had probably amused himself as a young man with the *demi-monde* of Rome and Naples. Merimée's Carmen would have been beyond his ken: her heartlessness and the squalor of her life and surroundings would have shocked him and given his sentimental attachment to Mediterranean life a rude shock. On the whole, then, he was well served by Meilhac and Halévy.

The Overture is blatant and tawdry, sparing no sensibilities and leaving nothing to the imagination. Here is the bright, picture-postcard colouring of Southern Spain, the extrovert bull-fight music, and the facile swing of a popular entertainment: this is not evocation, not poetry, but realism. The orchestration suggests a military band, the wood-wind shrill, and the brass leaving no doubt as to the strong beat of the bar. The middle section (later in the opera, the song of the toreador) has a *canaille* swagger, an outrageous self-confidence: and it is only at the end of the overture that realism gives way to evocation, journalist's prose to poetry. Beneath a tremolando of the strings, clarinets, bassoons, cornet and violoncelli announce the phrase which sums up the tragedy even before it has been played.

Ex.28

Twice it rises and falls again, but the third time it mounts to a climax there is a sudden break, silence, and after four introductory bars the curtain rises on the first act. The guard is lounging in front of the guard-house on a square in Seville, the right of which is taken up by a cigarette factory. The usual desultory life of the plaza is going on round the soldiers, who spend their time watching the passers-by, smoking and chatting. Bizet's opening chorus suggests the hot, lazy, good-natured atmosphere. The brigadier, Morales (an invention of the librettists), is as bored as the rest, until he sees a country girl obviously in search of someone, and not daring to speak to the soldiers. Micaela's entry is marked by a sudden break in the chorus, three bars transition in the wood-wind and then a light, tripping figure in the violins, picked out with a sustained phrase, first on the bassoons and then in the horns, while Morales draws his companions' attention to the girl. He asks her what she wants, and she replies that she is looking for the brigadier, Don José. She is disappointed that he is not there, but Morales tells her that he will come when the guard is changed: meanwhile, will she not come into the guard-room and wait? He is gallant: and the horn pedal gives his invitation a warmth and a tenderness which frightens the rather self-conscious Micaela, who frees herself from the soldiers who have surrounded her and, with a flirtatious ' Au revoir, messieurs les soldats!', she is away, accompanied by a whirling succession of trills on the strings. Philosophically the gallant Morales settles down again to watching the life of the square, and the nonchalant opening chorus returns, after an exquisite transition passage, as the orchestra gradually loses its colour and sinks again to quiet humdrum.

A cornet in the distance announces the changing of the guard, and the soldiers stretch themselves and begin to line up. The relieving company is preceded by a horde of urchins who march on to the stage in mock-military order, accompanied by a toy march. Two flutes begin and gradually they are joined by an occasional flourish from the cornet, and supported here and there by chords on the strings pizzicato. The march fills out and develops into a chorus sung by the urchins, the brass adding a mock pomposity and the excitement growing as an interior horn pedal and decorative figures on the wood-wind add to the orchestral volume. At the head of the new company are Lieutenant Zuniga and the Brigadier Don José. Morales tells José of the country girl who was looking for him, and from his description José recognises Micaela, the sweetheart he left behind in Navarre when he joined the army. The urchins repeat their chorus and begin to move off, their march disappearing gradually from the orchestra as they leave the stage. Zuniga asks José about the cigarette factory and the girls who work there. Are they as beautiful and as loose as they are said to be? José is not interested, and Zuniga twits him with his fidelity to his sweetheart. As the clock strikes and the girls begin to come out of the factory, the plaza fills with the young gallants of Seville: José sits on one side, in front of the guard-house, making himself a chain. The young men in the crowd, lovers or would-be lovers of the factory girls, plead their suits in a chorus whose sweetness and restraint would melt any heart. It is beautifully orchestrated, the wood-wind occasionally touching the strings with colour and the oboe following the voices in the closing phrases. As the cigarette girls stream out of the factory and the crowd comments on them, strings and harp start a flowing accompaniment figure, while first flute and clarinet, then oboe and bassoon, and finally violins and violas have a swaying and mounting phrase that rises and falls until, after a few bars' orchestral interlude, the girls themselves (divided into first and second soprani) start their chorus— graceful, nonchalant and disturbing to the senses. Lovers' words are as flimsy as the smoke that rises from a cigarette, they say: and the middle section is gay and quietly cynical in contrast with the voluptuous opening phrases which are repeated at the end. Then Carmen appears, heralded by a phrase which is the tragic phrase of the overture in another rhythm.

Ex.29

The young gallants who wooed the factory girls so sweetly now turn to Carmen and press her, with far more vehemence and less circumspection, for an answer to their several suits. Her first look is at Don José, the only man unconscious of her arrival, and she fobs off her admirers with a coquettish answer and breaks straight into the Habañera.

Bizet is said to have rewritten the Habañera thirteen times in order to please Galli-Marié, who was the first interpreter of the rôle of Carmen: and at the end to have said viciously: ' They wanted trash: well, they've got it.' The final version is based on a Spanish or Spanish-American tango: and if it is trash, it is at least admirably apt. It contains Carmen's philosophy of life, if anything so perversely capricious can be called a philosophy. When it is over she is surrounded by admirers, pressing their claims; but, true to her philosophy, she has eyes only for José, who has sat the whole time unmoved, intent on making his chain. Clarinets and violas announce the tragic phrase from the overture in its original form, as Carmen starts to walk nonchalantly towards the factory, then suddenly turns, walks straight up to José, takes the flower from her dress, and throws it in his face. The crowd surrounds him, humming a phrase of the Habañera—' Si tu ne m'aimes pas, je t'aime ', and then bursting into laughter at his astonishment. The clock sounds in the factory and the girls start to return, as the orchestra bursts into a wild phrase which foretells the tragedy and suffering which, as it were, already begotten, will come to birth in due time.

Left alone, José tries to recover himself. ' Cette fleur-là m'a fait l'effet d'une balle qui m'arrivait ', he mutters: if there are witches, Carmen must be one. But he is interrupted by the arrival of Micaela, who brings a letter from his mother and a small sum of money to supplement his pay. The duet which follows was one of the few numbers of the opera which was unequivocally praised when

Carmen was first produced: it was found charming, fresh, and pure in contrast with the brutality and moral depravity of the rest of the work. Nowadays the situation is reversed and the duet is found by many critics banal, sentimental and supremely false to Merimée. False to Merimée it certainly is: and no one can deny that Micaela is maddeningly arch in her manner of giving José the kiss sent by his mother. But Bizet has made José's devotion to his mother quite real: it is the love of a very weak and malleable son, but none the less love, warm, tender and simple. He is carried away from the present back to his home and his mother; and if his transports are rather sentimental in

Ma mère, je la vois . . .

Oui, je revois mon village!

O souvenirs d'autrefois, doux souvenirs du pays! they are perfectly true to type and show no more than an amiable weakness. To have written nothing, or profoundly moving music, would have been a false characterisation of José. The thought of Carmen interrupts him for a moment and the horns, which Bizet has used to give warmth and a kind of distant nostalgic home-calling to Jose's memories, sound suddenly sinister, with Carmen's tragic theme above them:

Ex.30

Micaela is puzzled by José's distress, but he reassures her and the duet is protracted, with certainly too much repetition. She tells him to read the letter, while she is away, and she will return: he reads and finds that his mother begs him to take Micaela as his wife. He is just reassuring her mentally, and consigning Carmen to oblivion and perdition, when there is a loud sound of quarrelling from the cigarette factory. Zuniga comes out of the guard-house and is immediately surrounded by two rival factions of women, explaining their two views of the quarrel and asking him to punish the culprit. Either Carmen insulted and struck Manuelita or Manuelita insulted and struck Carmen. Bizet catches perfectly the atmosphere of the quarrel, the chattering women,

Ex. 31

La Ma-nuel-i-ta di - sait — Et ré-pé-tait à voix hau - te

and Zuniga's impatience. He details José to go with two men and see what has happened: and is then besieged again by the chatter, threats and curses of the rival factions. Finally, the guard clears the plaza and, as the orchestra plays the wild theme to which Carmen disappeared before, she is led out of the factory by José, who reports that it is she who has wounded Manuelita. Carmen is perfectly calm, and

when Zuniga asks her what she has to say, she
starts humming insolently and declares she will say
nothing, even under torture. Zuniga tells her to
stop her humming, but she starts again and only
interrupts herself, when the rival faction call for her
to be taken off to prison, to strike out at the woman
nearest to her. Then she starts her impudent
humming again, staring coquettishly at Zuniga.
He is attracted, and her flirting mollifies him: but
he orders her off to prison, telling José to tie her
hands together. The women troop back into the
factory, Zuniga goes back to the guard-house.

Alone with José, Carmen plays her last and most
effective card. ' Tu feras tout ce que je veux, et
cela parce que tu m'aimes ', she tells him: the
charm has told, the flower has done its work. José
is furious and tells her to be silent: but he is badly
shaken. Carmen's Seguidilla, sung first for herself
and increasingly directed at him, rouses him to a
fury of jealous passion. She has just got rid of a
lover, she tells him—

> Mon pauvre cœur (très consolable)
> Mon cœur est libre comme l'air!
> J'ai des galants à la douzaine,
> Mais ils ne sont pas à mon gré.
> Voici la fin de la semaine:
> Qui veut m'aimer? Je l'aimerai.

and she paints the picture of drinking together in
Lillas Pastia's tavern, twitting him with his rank,
low but ' good enough for a gipsy '. By the time she
has finished, he is desperate and ready to do anything for her. Micaela, with her pigtail and her blue
skirt, her home-made charm and her coquettish
prudery, is quite forgotten. The Seguidilla is a

perfect piece of characterisation, lightly and beautifully orchestrated, and enough to turn any man's
head. As Zuniga comes out of the guard-house and
the theme of the quarrel is heard again in the
orchestra, Carmen gives José his instructions. On
the way to prison she will push him over and he is
to fall; she will see to the rest. The rendezvous is
Lillas Pastia's tavern: José is not likely to forget it.
Humming the habañera and smiling insolently at
Zuniga, she makes ready to start, surrounded by
the soldiers and guarded by José. The orchestra
takes up the habañera, with an air half mocking,
half sinister.

Ex.32

There is a sudden break, Carmen knocks over
José and is gone in a moment, and the act closes
with the quarrel theme, now in the major, ricochet-
ting across the orchestra.

As in *L'Arlésienne*, there is an entr'acte between the
acts, a bassoon solo, supported by strings and drum

which give it a soldierly air, yet with something solitary and nocturnal about it. There is a charming middle section, where strings and wood-wind answer each other antiphonally, and then the solo returns, this time in the clarinet, supported by a staccato bassoon.

Act II is laid in Lillas Pastia's tavern, and the curtain goes up on a gipsy dance, flute and piccolo in thirds racing and whirling above an accompaniment of pizzicato strings and harp, which give the effect of guitars. At first Carmen sings by herself, then she is joined by her gipsy friends, Mercedes and Frasquita (inventions of the librettists again). The atmosphere becomes more and more orgiastic, the dances wilder and faster, then suddenly cease. The tavern is closing and Zuniga, who has been watching Carmen dance, asks her to go with him. She refuses, and learns casually that José, who has been in prison for conniving at her escape, is free again. In the distance there are sounds of cheers, and before Lillas Pastia has time to close, Escamillo, a favourite bull-fighter from Granada, enters, escorted by a large crowd of admirers carrying torches. Zuniga and the other guests greet him and drink to his health; and he answers with the famous ' Toreador's Song ', an amiable and effective piece of vulgarity, psychologically irreproachable (Bizet even marks the refrain ' avec fatuité '), and bearing the true accent of the popular hero. At the end Frasquita, Mercedes and Carmen try their amorous tricks on Escamillo, and he responds to each in turn: but it is Carmen he takes aside afterwards, asking her her name and what she would say to being loved by him. She answers coldly, but with

more than a hint of provocation: Zuniga is jealous,
and though he leaves with Escamillo, he tells her
that he will return. After the bull-fighter and his
party have gone, two men enter, Remendado and
le Dancaïre.

The tavern is a smugglers' rendezvous, and these
two are known to Carmen and her friends who
work with them. The quintet which follows, in
which the men ask the women's help in an ' affair '
they are planning, is a model of operatic idiocy, so
far as the words are concerned. There are endless
repetitions and the whole matter, which could have
been settled in a dozen bars of recitative, is expanded
into a concerted number of over one hundred bars.
But they are some of the most brilliant ever written
by Bizet, full of verve, laughter, good humour and
brilliance, orchestrated largely for the wood-wind,
with rocketing scales and crisp rhythms. Mercedes
and Frasquita agree to go with the smugglers:
Carmen refuses. A horn pedal with woodwind
echoes from the quintet quivering above it, half
veils her refusal. The two men plead with her: the
women ask her reason. And for the first time she
shows another side of herself: in the middle of the
good-humoured *bonhomie* she suddenly becomes
pensive, serious.

Ex.33

Her avowal is greeted with laughter and incredulity. Remendado and le Dancaïre are ironical. Carmen accepts their irony and repeating their music apologises—love must go before duty. The others know their Carmen and only make a half-hearted attempt to dissuade her. The scene ends with a pianissimo recapitulation of the quintet; and just as Carmen is being twitted with the absence of her lover, the theme of the entr'acte is heard in the wings, sung by a tenor voice which comes gradually nearer. Le Dancaïre begs Carmen to try and persuade her lover to join the smugglers, and she agrees. As the voice comes nearer still, the others leave Carmen. José appears, surprisingly gay after his two months in prison, which seem to have given him self-confidence and to have redoubled his passion for Carmen. This is a weak spot in the librettists' psychology: the José of Act I would have been chastened and frightened by his experience and surely have returned to his Micaela when he got out of prison. He is jealous when he hears that Carmen has been dancing for other guests of Lillas Pastia, so she takes the castanets and dances for him to her own accompaniment. José is enthralled and does not at first hear the retreat which is being sounded in the distance from the barracks, mingling, almost imperceptibly, with Carmen's song. But as it grows louder and is at last unmistakable, he becomes uncomfortable and tries to interrupt her. He has got to go back to barracks. She is furious with him, mocks his pusillanimity, and finally tells him to go. He pleads with her, but she will not listen to him, until he shows her the flower which she threw at him and he has kept ever since. The tragic theme from the overture appears in the cor anglais and leads to José's 'flower song', his one lyrical outburst before he is carried away on a sea of passion which is too strong for him and can only end in his utter wreck. At the close of the song there is a modulation which shocked the critics by its boldness: and it is interesting to compare it with its predecessor in *La Jolie Fille de Perth*.

Ex. 34ᵃ

Ex. 34ᵇ

Carmen sees that she has got José in her power and, with her promise to le Dancaïre in her mind, she begins to play with him as a cat plays with a mouse. Beneath a pedal G the chromatic scale rises and falls (cp. ex. 17) as Carmen leads up to her demand. José pleads, but with less and less conviction, his duty and the claims of honour. Carmen answers by painting the liberty and freedom from restraint of the smuggler's life, away in the mountains. Finally, in a last effort of self-assertion, José defies her: and he is just about to go when there is a knocking at the door and Zuniga's voice is heard asking to be admitted.

A sinister passage for clarinets and bassoons over a drum roll, a crash, and Zuniga breaks down the door and stands in the room. He twits Carmen with taking the common soldier when she already has the officer, turns to José with a 'Get out', and is surprised to meet a flat refusal and a challenge. As they fight the smugglers creep back and leap on Zuniga, who is overpowered and has to give in. Carmen mocks him, while Remendado and le Dancaïre hold a pistol to his head and ask him politely to follow them. Zuniga takes it in good part: he cannot very well refuse, but he swears to get even with them later. As Carmen turns to José and asks him if he, too, will follow them, there is a reminiscence in the orchestra of the foregoing scene, where she painted the joys of a smuggler's life in the mountains. José assents half-heartedly, and the act closes with a full chorus, surging forward to a great cry of 'Freedom', on which the curtain falls.

In the entr'acte which follows there are a few moments' respite before the net of the tragedy begins to close over Carmen and José. A flute solo, over harp accompaniment, carries us back to the world of *L'Arlésienne* (cp. also the Minuet in *Jolie Fille de Perth*): the clarinets and then the horns add warmth and richness, but do not detract from the perfect tranquillity of the atmosphere. Act III is laid in the sierra, and the entr'acte seems to express something of the stillness and purity of the mountian before Carmen, José and the smugglers break in on it with their all-too-human passions.

Bizet opens the act with a pianissimo march, the flutes accompanied by the lower strings pizzicato, giving an air of eeriness and unreality to the scene. As the procession of smugglers enters, the march is heard in the strings: and the bassoons, plodding in thirds beneath the theme, preserve the clandestine atmosphere. With the trombones and the entry of the voices (tenors and basses in octave unison) the last touches are added: and the sextet (Mercedes, Frasquita, Carmen, José, Remendado and le Dancaïre) merely elaborates the picture. There is a rather brighter note in the distinctly Meyerbeerian major section of the sextet, which emphasises the carefree existence of the outlaws, gay for all its dangers: and the plodding march returns. José is gloomy, thinking too late of the mother whose confidence he has betrayed. Carmen laughs at his sentimentality, and tells him to go back to her. They start to quarrel, quietly as though it were a habit; but in the orchestra the tragic theme warns the audience that the quarrel is serious, and Carmen is only half in fun when she suggests that perhaps José will kill her one day. The whole cortège settles down to rest, and Frasquita and Mercedes take a pack of cards to tell their fortunes The wood-wind sounds bleakly over the horn pedal and the regular trill of the strings. (See ex. 35.)

119

Ex. 35

From the cards the two girls discover very much
what they want. Frasquita is romantic and foresees
a young lover who adores her and a wild, outlaw
life with him in the sierra. Mercedes is a realist and
sees a rich old man who marries her, soon dies, and
leaves her a rich widow. They are not too serious,
and thoroughly enjoy the game. Carmen tries her
hand in silence: only her version of the tragic theme
is heard in the orchestra and her muttered words:
' La mort! j'ai bien lu . . . moi d'abord, ensuite
lui . . . pour tous les deux, la mort! ' And then
she breaks into a sombre and passionate monologue,
full of fatalism, accompanied by the strings which
are later amplified by the trombone, as the thought
of death, its pitilessness and inevitability, becomes
more and more prominent. She is interrupted by
the gay chatter of Mercedes and Frasquita: and
the scene ends with the repetition of their duet.
Finally, le Dancaïre summons the whole company
to move on: it is the women's business to distract
the attention of the excise officers on the pass, while
the men get the contraband through unnoticed.

The women are quite prepared for their part, and there is a gay, swaggering, self-confident chorus which enlivens the spirits of the whole band. José is to be left on guard, hidden on the ridge, and to shoot any intruder on sight. The smugglers move off with their women, José takes up his post out of sight, and for a moment the stage is empty.

A tender phrase in the oboe and a timid flutter in the strings announce Micaela, who has come in search of José. Then horns and a beautiful sweeping figure in the violoncelli introduce the air in which she expresses her fear, her determination to be brave, and her feeling of complete inadequacy in the face of smugglers, gipsies, and a José whom she can hardly hope to recognise as her old sweetheart. Half prayer, half monologue, Micaela's air forms the greatest imaginable contrast with the foregoing music, and by it she more than redeems the coquetry of her behaviour in Act I. At last she catches a glimpse of José: but as she sees him he puts his rifle to his shoulders, seems to aim at her and fires, only a moment after she has taken refuge behind a rock. But it was not at her that José was firing. As Micaela disappears Escamillo walks coolly on to the scene, followed by José, to whom he explains the reason of his coming. He is in love with a gipsy who is with the smugglers, Carmen by name. She is tiring of her present lover, a soldier who deserted for her sake—Carmen's loves seldom last six months. Having discovered all he wants to know, José discloses himself and challenges Escamillo. The situation is summed up in a very weak and uninteresting duet between the two men, which would be far better omitted: and they set to with their knives.

Escamillo is being worsted and José is just about to
stab him when Carmen reappears with the smugglers
and saves Escamillo, who thanks her and, turning
mockingly to José, offers to renew the quarrel any
day he chooses. Then he goes, after inviting any
of the company who care to come to watch him in his
next bull-fight at Seville. His words and his way of
looking at Carmen infuriate José.

Ex.36
ESCAMILLO

Et qui m'aime y vien-dra___ Et qui

m'aime y vien-dra_____

But Escamillo is gone and le Dancaïre summons
the smugglers to move on when Remendado catches
sight of Micaela crouching behind her rock and
brings her forward. She turns straight to José, who
is terribly moved by the sight of her, and gives him

again the message from his mother. Carmen urges
José to go: but he sees in her advice merely a ruse
to get rid of him. For the first time he sees red and
there is murder in the air.

Ex. 37

JOSÉ

Dût - il m'en coû - ter la vi - e Non, Car-

- men je ne par - ti - rai pas!

Micaela, in despair, plays her last card. Flutes and
clarinets mark the change of atmosphere, as she
explains that José's mother is dying and longs to
see him again before it is too late. José is won: but
the theme of tragedy sounds in the orchestra as he
tells Carmen that they will meet again. In the
distance Escamillo's song rings out, trolled down
the mountain side. As Carmen runs to catch a last
glimpse of him, José rushes to prevent her: and the
curtain falls on the chorus with which the act
opened, as the smugglers move off in one direction,
José and Micaela in another.

The entr'acte which follows is a masterpiece of
evocation. A single oboe standing out above a rough
accompaniment in strings and accentuated by the
rattle of a *tambour de Basque*, is interrupted by wild
flurrying figures on the flute and clarinets an octave
apart; and as it develops the strings rush and trill,
breaking up the theme again and again, till it finally

dies away. There is something inexpressibly tragic, boding ill, like a single bird hovering over a boiling sea, which is never seen though its waves occasionally leap up with a whistling roar. It is a dance of death, with a gipsy flavour, nakedly tragic.

The curtain goes up on the scene outside the Seville bullring, packed with an excited and expectant crowd, painted by Bizet with extraordinary brilliance; and there is a moment when one is transported to another crowd, waiting outside the Kremlin not for a favourite bull-fighter but for a new tsar.

Ex. 38

With the return of the music of the overture the procession of toreros, chulos and banderilleros begins, each group being hailed by the crowd with new cries of delight, until finally the *Espada* or toreador himself appears, and the whole crowd breaks into the chorus of Escamillo's song. He appears with Carmen on his arm, languid with love and gorgeously dressed. His words to Carmen before he disappears into the ring make it clear that she is his mistress: their tone is warm, tender, almost anxious, quite different from his former Don Juan bravado. As the alcalde and alguazils appear, the crowd follows them into the stadium, and Carmen is left alone with Mercedes and Frasquita, who stay behind a moment. They warn her that José is about: and in the orchestra appears an apparently innocent theme

which is repeated again and again and seems to acquire a note that is the very essence of danger, the dominant pedal and the flute phrase which circles round the dominant expressing perfectly the feeling of impending disaster beneath all the gaiety and glamour of the scene. Carmen refuses to be warned and Mercedes and Frasquita leave her. From the stadium come phrases of the overture, violently interrupted by a harsh, descending chromatic scale, and gradually dying away. José appears. He starts to plead, but Carmen refuses to listen to him. He will forget the past, he says: they will go abroad and start life again together. She is firm, but not without pity at first: only his adoring importunity gets on her nerves, as it must when she has ceased to love him and her whole mind is taken up with the thought and love of another man. But José returns to his pleading, until her coldness suddenly seems to strike deathly chill into him.

She answers with a simple ' No ', which enrages
him and fires his jealousy and desperation. Carmen,
too, is gradually losing patience; and the cries of
excitement from the bull-ring turn her mind back
with redoubled strength to Escamillo: her one idea
is to get away from José into the stadium, to witness
her lover's victory. José asks her if she loves him,
and her passionate denial is drowned in another
burst of cheering. Now the tragic theme reappears,
as José grows beside himself, ceases to plead and
tries to use violence to make her go with him. Once
again her reply—her impatient ' *frappe-moi donc, ou
laisse-moi passer* '—is drowned in cheers. José
threatens her for the last time. She throws his ring

in his face and from the ring there comes the echoing toreador chorus, announcing Escamillo's victory, as José hurls himself on Carmen and stabs her. As the crowd pours out, he gives himself up

Ex.41

and the curtain falls.

CHAPTER VII

' YESTERDAY I heard for the twentieth time—will you believe me?—Bizet's masterpiece. How a work of this kind makes better men of us! One becomes a masterpiece oneself. . . . This music seems to me to be perfect. It comes forward with lightness, suppleness . . . " light-footed are the gods ". . . . It is cruel, exquisite, full of fatalism: and yet it remains popular . . . its refinement is the refinement of a race. . . . It is rich, precise. It constructs, it organises, it is finished. Have the accents of a more tragic grief ever been heard on the stage? And how are they achieved? Without posturing, without welching, without the fraud of the grand style. . . . This music has the quality of warm countries: the dryness of the air, its *limpidezza*. In it there is expressed a different sensuality, a different sensibility, another gaiety. This music is gay, but with a gaiety which is neither French nor German. Its gaiety is truly African: it contains a fatality, joy is short-lived, sudden, without indulgence. Bizet is to be envied for having had the courage of this sensibility which had never hitherto been expressed in the music of civilised Europe—I mean this burning, brazen, southern sensibility. . . . I repeat, this music has made a better man of me. *Music must be Mediterraneanised!* Back to nature, health, gaiety, youth, *virtue!* . . . '—(NIETZSCHE.)

Carmen embodied for Nietzsche the antithesis of all that Wagner meant to him, the antithesis of what

128

Ruskin called ' the foggy taverns of the North '. Now, after more than half a century, what is conventional and what is truly original in *Carmen* stands out distinctly: that Bizet was not completely original is no longer held against him, his place in the tradition of French opera is now both clear and honourable. There is no other opera like *Carmen*, and to have constructed a unique work on the scaffolding provided by Meilhac and Halévy is a remarkable feat. There is no question of a recreation of Merimée's characters nor of his story; there is no question even of a brilliant piece of exoticism. Bizet's characters are French in thought and feeling, neither gipsy nor Spanish. *Carmen* is a French opera to the core, inspired by a sympathetic admiration for southern, Mediterranean life certainly, but from the outside. Bizet writes of the South as Goethe in his *Roemische Elegien*, as Wolf in *Der Corregidor*. He never forgot his life at the Villa Médicis, and *Carmen* is the final justification of that extra year spent in Italy rather than in Germany.

Micaela, the most unmistakably French and nineteenth-century figure of the opera, would be out of place in Merimée, and those who resent her presence in *Carmen*, as an act of treachery to Merimée, are looking for something to which Bizet never pretended, which he was never capable of creating. Her charm is the conventional charm of contrast: by herself she would be simply insipid, but by the side of Carmen's heartlessness and amorality her unpretentious and ordinary traits—her conventional love of José, her horror of the whole outlaw life, even her coquetry and rather too conscious rectitude—have a charm and a dramatic rightness which even irritation cannot obscure. She is the only self-conscious figure in the whole work: the others are all spontaneous, unreflecting, and therein lies their attractiveness. Micaela is a bore, no doubt; but apart from a few needless exaggerations she is a true bore, and without her presence to act as a foil the quality of the other characters would not stand out as it does. She is the one representative of ordinary life, and to say that ordinary life may be tame and boring is not to say that it does not exist.

Nietzsche was blind to all but the feline, cruel, fatalistic aspect of *Carmen*: he was the typical over-civilised man in search of strong sensations, tortured by *ennui* and in violent revolt against the qualities of Micaela, which are the very qualities of settled, civilised life which made his own existence possible. But he did no more than exaggerate an element which is really present in *Carmen*. There is a tough-ness and heartlessness, almost a brutality, which grows with each act until it entirely dominates Act IV; the quality which perhaps more than any other strikes the Northern European in South-ern life, a complete absence of kindliness, of the spirit which makes for compromise and *laissez-faire*, an extraordinary concentration on the indivi-dual's business of living untouched by that tendency to dream and to speculate about ultimate ends which makes the fogs of the North somehow more endurable than the warmth and light of the South. Carmen's song over the cards is fatalistic, not despairing: she accepts the idea of death without emotional agonising, and this is foreign to us, unnatural. When Frasquita and Mercedes warn her in Act IV that José is on her tracks, they are cool and unemotional: they warn her, but in the last resort her life is her own affair, one hears them say, and they for their part do not wish to miss the bullfight. To the northerner they are indifferent, heartless; there is nothing to appeal to in them. It was this which fascinated Nietzsche, rather as it would fascinate D. H. Lawrence, and for the same reason. Perpetually appealing and needing to appeal to the kindliness and sympathy of others, such men despise both themselves and those who listen to their appeals. They have something in common with the José, not of Merimée certainly, but of Meilhac and Halévy; for he is essentially dependent. It is psychologically true that he should love both Micaela and Carmen: Micaela was the woman for him, and it was inevitable that he should be fascinated by Carmen. That is his tragedy, that and the characterlessness which makes him the slave and not the master of his circumstances. The gravest fault of Bizet's librettists is not to have introduced Micaela at all, as many critics have said, but to have introduced her in Act I, so that José should be conscious of the antagonism between her claims and those of Carmen, and then in Act II to have sent José after a month in prison straight back, with a swaggering self-confidence which he completely lacked in Act I, to Carmen, whom he would most naturally have forgotten while he was cooling his heels in prison. It is true that he soon weakens and becomes recognisable as the José of Act I, but it is a blemish on the act and on the story as a whole.

Carmen was performed on March 3, 1875, and was not a success. The exact extent of its failure has been much disputed: but Bizet was certainly very disappointed and disheartened, for he had been pleased with his score and had foreseen a great popular success. As it was, he fell, as always, between two stools: apart from the moral disapprobation aroused by the libretto, he was blamed on the one hand for excessive harmonic harshness, on the other for vulgarity and too much truckling to the taste of the public. In the midst of the scandal and discussion he suddenly died, exactly three months after the first night. Ernest Guiraud, his close friend since the early days in Rome, spent the evening of May 30 with Bizet. 'It was the eve of his departure for Bougival', he wrote, 'and I had gone round to see him after dinner. He asked me to play him some of *Piccolino* which I was just beginning. I sat down at the piano, but I had hardly played a few bars when he put his hand on my shoulder. "One moment", he said, "I can't hear anything with this ear: I will go to the other side". This was said in a feeble voice, and as if he were in pain, so that I started when he spoke and turned round quickly. I did not recognise the Bizet I had always known, full of energy and youth; at that moment he looked sickly and in pain, and I was struck by a momentary vision, as fugitive as it was horrible.' Bizet had been thoroughly worn out by the rehearsals of *Carmen* and was unwell at the end of March. He hoped that the rest and quiet of Bougival would restore him, and the first night there (May 31) he slept well. During the night of June 1 he woke with a start, with a feeling of suffocation so intense that his wife summoned the doctor and their friend and neighbour Delaborde, the pianist. The doctor was reassuring and told Mme. Bizet not to worry herself (or him) if there

should be another attack. The next night the same
thing happened again, and Bizet was in such pain
that his wife did, in fact, send for the doctor.
By the time he came Bizet was already dead. From
the symptoms it seems fairly clear that he died of a
heart attack, brought on by years of overwork, and
more especially by the trouble and disappointment of
Carmen. At the time the causes of death given were
'purulent resorption', an embolism or a quinsy.
He had always been subject to tonsilitis; even from
Rome (March 1858) he had written home that
'everyone advises me to have my tonsils out: I
must consider it'. But it is difficult to reconcile the
accounts of his death with anything so comparatively simple and localised as quinsy, although acute
tonsilitis often neglected may well have weakened
his already delicate organism. He died at midnight,
as the curtain went down on the thirty-third performance of *Carmen*. Galli-Marié, who was playing
the name part, had arrived at the theatre earlier in
the evening in an appalling state of nervous pros-
tration, with an overwhelming sense of impending
disaster which she could not explain, bursting into
tears when du Locle tried to calm her. The next
morning the telegram announcing Bizet's death was
pinned outside the theatre.

It is almost impossible to foresee what Bizet might
have done had he lived, but it is certain that the
self-confidence which the ultimate success of
Carmen would have given him was the quality
which he had hitherto most lacked. He might very
well have lived until 1900 and heard the early works
of Debussy and Ravel. Debussy was indeed very
nearly his exact complement and one critic has

found in *Pelléas* the perfect antithesis to *Carmen*—
' tout en dehors, toute lumière, toute vie, sans
ombre, sans dessous: l'autre tout interiéure, toute
baignée de lumière crépuscule, tout enveloppée de
silence '. That the strain of weakness and over-
pliability in Bizet's nature would have led him to
more and more compromise with public taste is a
not easily warrantable prophecy made by those who
trace this trait back to his early youth and see little
but the expression of an ordinary though gifted
careerist in his letters from Rome.

As it was, *Carmen* set a new fashion in opera, a
fashion for directness and economy, almost for
brutality of statement and for realistic or ' powerful '
themes, which had hitherto not appeared on the
operatic stage. To have inspired *Cavalleria rusticana*
and *Pagliacci* is perhaps not a great boast; but
Mascagni and Leoncavallo were essential if Italian
music was to escape from the shadow of Verdi.

In Puccini, too, the French element which com-
bined with the Italian to make him the typically
Latin composer of the second rate, was the *Carmen*
element: and what worth there is in *Bohème* and
Tosca is very largely French. Puccini's dramatic gift
is absolutely unlike, in quality as well as in quantity,
that of Verdi. It is quick-moving and small-scale,
where Verdi's is measured, for all its violence, and
grand. Carmen's fatalism degenerated with Puccini
to pathos, the cruelty and exquisiteness, which
Nietzsche found in Bizet's music, became sadism
and foppishness. *Carmen* had nothing but unworthy
descendants in the direct line. *Djamileh* was thought
highly enough of by Gustav Mahler to be revived
in Vienna, but since then few conductors outside

France have tried to revive it with any success. The tragedy of Bizet does not lie in the opposition he met in his lifetime, for he had a reasonable share of success. He was a great musician, and all his later works show an extraordinary musical instinct and a fineness of ear in orchestration which have not often been equalled and very seldom surpassed. His tragedy lay in the fact that he developed late and died young, so that he had only a few years of maturity. His gifts, even when fully developed, were unspectacular, for they were typically French and, for that very reason, easy to under-estimate. Even *Carmen* has its detractors: but so long as opera is heard by more than professional critics, Bizet's name will be known all over the world.

BIBLIOGRAPHY

BELLAIGUE, C. *Bizet*. Paris: 1891.
GALABERT, E. *Georges Bizet*. Paris: 1877.
GAUTHIERS-VILLARS, A. *Bizet (Musiciens célèbres)*.
IMBERT, H. *Portraits et études*. Paris: 1894.
ISTEL, E. *Bizet und ' Carmen.'* Stuttgart: 1927.
LANDORMY, P. *Georges Bizet (Maîtres de la Musique)*.
Paris: 1924.
Lettres de Georges Bizet (Preface by Louis Gandérax).
Paris: 1907.
Lettres à un ami, 1865-72. Paris: 1909.
NIETZSCHE, F. *Randglossen zu Bizets ' Carmen '*. (Ed.
H. Daffner: 1912.)
PARKER, D. C. *Georges Bizet, his Life and Works*.
London: 1926.
PIGOT, C. *Bizet et son œuvre*. Paris: 1886.
RABE, J. *Georges Bizet*. Stockholm: 1925.
VOSS, P. *Bizet (Reclams Universal Bibliothek, 1899)*.
WEISSMANN, A. *Bizet (Die Musik, 1907)*.